THE SMOKING PARADOX

THE SMOKING PARADOX

Public Regulation in the Cigarette Industry

Gideon Doron

State University of
New York at Binghamton

Abt Books
Cambridge, Massachusetts

ACE-9601

Michael Connolly, Acquisitions Editor
Nancy Miner, Production Editor
Judy Ranan, Book Design
Robert J. Steinberg, Title Page Photograph
Deborah Greene, Typesetting
Michael Roe, Production Manager

Library of Congress Catalog Card Number 79-50400

Printed in the United States of America

ISBN: 0-89011-531-1

TO SHIRA AND AERAN

Contents

List of Figures

List of Tables

Foreword

William H. Riker
University of Rochester

In the political consciousness of twentieth century Americans, two notable falsehoods distort the operation of government. One is the notion that the force of government can make people better human beings. The other is the notion that this force can, entirely of itself and however unimaginatively applied, bring about a desired state of affairs.

Both these presuppositions underlie the regulatory action analyzed in this book. The regulation of advertising for cigarettes was, in large part, undertaken simply to make smokers better people in the sense that they might become more careful about the state of their own health. This regulation was blithely based on the expectation that because its intention was to discourage smoking, it would actually do so.

The great merit of Professor Doron's analysis is that it shows, in the concrete case of a particular regulation, just how misleading these presuppositions are. The prohibition of cigarette advertising on television was actually followed by increased sales of cigarettes. Even more striking, the prohibition enormously strengthened the financial resources of the producers so that they have presumably become better able to distribute their wares, hardly a circumstance that discourages smoking.

Professor Doron's study adds one more piece to the swiftly growing body of evidence that, contrary to the sentimental and simpleminded expectations of reformers, society cannot easily enforce goodness, nor can social outcomes be changed by fiat. This work offers us, therefore, one more caution against being misled by ideologues who perpetuate fallacies.

And the caution is necessary because these fallacies are ideology in the true sense, namely the justification of a special interest. In this case, the interests served are those of some bureaucrats and, especially, those of certain lobbies of reformers who prefer to devote the charitable contributions they receive to medical investigations, rather than to making television commercials and buying television time to state their case.

My hope is that studies like Professor Doron's will increasingly reveal to citizens the fallacies involved in the ideology of regulation. Perhaps we can then turn democratic government away from regulation by fiat and back to what such a form of government does best; using persuasion or the rule-making power of government to give private persons an incentive to act in the public interest. Professor Doron illustrates that when the government provided incentives (through the Fairness Doctrine) for private advertising against cigarettes, so that some citizens could without using force persuade others to quit smoking, then smoking in fact declined. The action of government was efficacious, not primarily because of the legal force involved in the rule making, but rather because the incentives offered were cleverly and indirectly arranged to encourage private interests, acting for individual advantage, to produce a socially beneficial outcome.

Acknowledgements

In the process of researching and preparing this book for publication, I have profited from contacts with many scholars: political scientists, economists and students of marketing. I would like to express my deepest gratitude to three individuals in particular: William Riker, my mentor, Bruce Jacubs and Dan Horsky, all from the University of Rochester. I would also like to thank Richard Hofferbert, Richard Kronick, Peter Lemieux and H. L. Nieburg for their critical comments and suggestions. My appreciation is extended to Jerry Myers for his technical assistance and to Shirley Stacconi for her skilled typing. Finally, I offer thanks to my wife Marcia, who was in many ways the coauthor of this book.

Gideon Doron
Binghamton, New York
November 1978

ONE

Introduction

ONE

DEFINITION OF THE PROBLEM

The cultural foundation of the American political economy has made the allocation of goods by the private market a key societal choice function. In recent decades, however, a growing awareness of imperfections in the operation of the free market has resulted in attempts by the public sector to remedy some of the shortcomings of this mechanism. One means of correction is the regulation of an industry's activities, and laymen, as well as policy analysts, now recognize a growing trend toward regulation of market activities. There has not been, however, a corresponding increase in knowledge relating to the causes and effects of such intervention.

Economists, long-time students of the market, have often concerned themselves with the effects of public intervention on the operation of the market. Although most studies direct their attention to what is considered an almost unique American phenomenon—the regulation of public utilities — the recent growing number of government regulations has stimulated investigation into the non-utility industries as well.[1] Social scientists' attraction to the issue may be a result of their concern with the environment, the quality of consumer products, or, in general, the quality of life. The effects of the various regulatory acts on society and their desirability — only partly explained by the economist — are the implicit concerns of this study.

In dealing with public regulations, a subclass of public policies, the following major questions should be raised:

1. Are they justified? (Given a particular market imperfection, will the regulations remedy it?)
2. Are they effective? (Do they achieve their stated or intended objectives? Furthermore, do the resulting social benefits outweigh their social costs?)
3. Who really benefits? (Does the public benefit more than industry?)

1

4. Do considerations of public information and practical politics
    come into conflict in the formulation and implementation of
    regulations?

This study will address these issues by considering a recent and
relatively uncomplicated regulatory activity — the U.S. federal
government's intervention in the private production, marketing and
consumption of cigarettes.

The federal government has passed at least three major regulatory acts relating to the cigarette industry and its products. They
are as follows:

1. The labelling requirements, first implemented in January
    1966, required a health warning to be printed on each pack-
    age of cigarettes sold. Later, a warning was also required to
    appear on every cigarette advertisement (Public Law 89-
    92, U.S.C. 1331-1339).
2. The Fairness Doctrine, advanced by the Federal Communica-
    tions Commission, guaranteed free broadcast time to anti-
    smoking forces and provided public assistance for anti-
    smoking commercials aired between the years 1968 and
    1970 (Communication Act 315(a), 47, U.S.C.).
3. The prohibition of television and radio commercials for
    cigarettes, implemented on January 2, 1971 (Public Law
    91-222, April 1, 1970).

This case study will show that there exist situations of intense
market competition where collusion is legally prohibited, but where
firms do, nonetheless, collude. At a political level, different firms in
the same industry (each firm assumed to be a profit maximizer)
are continually attempting to advance and acquire regulations which
will improve their own individual market situation. Public regulation
is usually just one episode in the dynamic process of conflict between the industry and groups outside it. Further, due to the politi-
cal-economic context of the American system, the conflict is often
a result of influences external to the production or consumption of
a given product. The existence of these not only leads to the articulation of demands on the government to regulate the industry but
often also serves as the normative basis for such governmental intervention in the market. The intervention is thus usually enforced
in the name of the "public interest."

The central thesis of this study is that public regulation is a sort of political solution to an actual or anticipated conflict between various groups (industry and others). The industry is forced to utilize political means to reach a solution which more often than not reflects the present "power" position of the different groups engaged in the conflict. The nature of the conflict, the stakes involved, the saliency of the policy issue, and the amount each group is ready to invest in the solution will determine, to a large degree, the character of the specific regulatory act.

As a corollary, it will be shown that as a consequence of an industry's being able (or forced) to move from the economic arena to the political one, regulations designed to ensure free economic competition (i.e., antitrust laws) may in fact breed or generate regulations that serve to limit the scope of such competition.

FORMAT OF THE STUDY

In the preceding discussion four major policy questions were formulated to guide the investigation, and the final chapter of this study will provide some answers to them. Chapter two is a historical review of the regulation of the cigarette industry. The third chapter is divided into two parts. In the first, the theoretical aspects of public regulations and the atmosphere of conflict from which they come are discussed. The dynamic nature of the political process of regulatory activity is also treated. The second part concentrates on the governmental regulation of oligopolistic industry, the cigarette industry serving as a case study. It is shown in particular that the prohibition of advertising cigarettes in the broadcasting media was fully to the advantage of the industry. Chapter four is an attempt to provide rigorous empirical support for the theoretical discussion advanced in Chapter three. To this end an econometric model is utilized.

TWO

Historical Survey of Public
Regulation in the Cigarette Industry

TWO

From the time that tobacco was first widely used, controversy has surrounded the practice of smoking and the proper legal response to it. Paradoxically, the popularity of cigarettes in the United States in this century was partially the unintended result of regulations imposed on other tobacco products and on the tobacco industry as a whole.

The scope and extent of government intervention in the market practices of the cigarette industry can be seen to have fluctuated through the years. There have been at least two phases in the evolution of a government attitude toward the cigarette industry. The first, labelled the "private good" period, is characterized by intervention resulting from unacceptable market practices of firms in the industry. The second phase, the "public good" period, is that in which the product itself, due to its harmful effects on health, has come into the congressional and regulatory commissions' purview. This chapter suggests that as the nature of the intervention changed from one period to another, the industry adjusted itself to the new circumstances and remained for the most part unaffected.

THE PRIVATE GOOD PERIOD

Public regulation of the tobacco industry was a concomitant of the introduction of the crop for commercial purposes in the early sixteenth century. Quotas were imposed on the acreage allowed for cultivating and growing the plants, restrictions were placed on exports, tobacco was taxed at the port of arrival, and so on.[1]

Reasons for these limitations were religious, personal and moral. Often the rationale was even expressed in terms of health: for example, James I issued a proclamation in 1619 prohibiting the planting of tobacco within England and Wales, justifying the legislation by claiming that English tobacco was "more crude, poisonous and dangerous for the bodies and health of our subjects than that

that comes from hotter climates" (i.e., the American colonies).[2] Of course, the king and his mercantilist advisors had a vested interest in such an enactment. The crown could ensure desired income by taxing the crop in a few established ports. Additional income was drawn from commercial entrepreneurs who paid dearly for the rights to a monopoly on importation.

In this period one may note with interest, but hardly with surprise, that this form of legislation created a black market. It was reported that as much tobacco was landed on out-of-the-way British beaches, then smuggled and sold, as came through customs.[3]

Laissez faire thinkers, who generally opposed government intervention in the market, were not particularly disturbed when tobacco was under public regulation. The unquestioned champion of this school, Adam Smith, expressed this attitude in *The Wealth of Nations:*

> [sugar, rum and] tobacco, are commodities which are no where necessaries of life, which have become objects of almost universal consumption, and which are therefore extremely proper subjects of taxation.[4]

Perhaps it was just such an attitude that allowed tobacco taxes to become a major source of income in "tax-free" America.[5] A tax was first levied in 1794, but since it gave rise to general discontent it was abandoned two years later. Excise taxes on tobacco were imposed between 1812 and 1816 and again during the Civil War. Because it helped ease the financial stress of that war and the ones that followed, the federal tax on tobacco products has been levied since then.[6] Today, moreover, there is no single state which does not levy an additional state tax on tobacco products. Many localities tax these products as well.

Paper-wrapped cigarettes were commercially available as early as the eighteenth century. By that time cigarettes were generally considered a "feminine" form of tobacco and usually consumed by women.[7] The internal revenue law did not ignore the new member of the family of tobacco products, and in 1864 a special tax on "cigarettes made of tobacco, enclosed in paper wrapper . . . " was imposed.[8] Cigarettes gained increased popularity, however, only in the first quarter of the present century. Many factors contributed to this increase, such as automatic manufacturing machinery which lowered prices and increased availability, improved paper quality, appearance of new tobacco types known as "bright" or "Virginia," etc. The enormous increase in cigarette consumption after 1910 may be attributed, in part, to the public health complaints in that era against chewing tobacco and its inevitable accompaniment, the cuspidor.[9] Cigarettes, an existing substitute, replaced chewing tobacco (and cigars) in prominence in the tobacco industry.

One year after the prohibition of alcohol in 1921 (an act which endured twelve years and brought widespread bootlegging, moon-shining, organized crime and contempt for the law in general), cigarettes were outlawed in fourteen states. In 1927 those laws were repealed, but laws against sales to minors remained on the statute books.[10] In addition to the social and moral problems created by cigarette prohibition, it failed to meet its explicit goal — to reduce the number of cigarettes smoked. The following data is consistent with the view that prohibition served only as a lure:[11]

Years	Average cigarette consumption per year (billion units)
1900-1909	4.2
1910-1919	24.3
1920-1929	80.0

Figure one is a comparison of per capita consumption of various tobacco products from the beginning of the century to 1948. Since forms of consumption vary from one tobacco product to another, all products are standardized in terms of the number of pounds of tobacco utilized. The reader cannot fail to observe the meteoric rise of cigarette consumption since the beginning of the century.

It is interesting to note, in passing, that the prohibition act banned the "manufacture, sale, or transportation of intoxicating liquors . . . " but not their consumption.[12] Regulation of the cigarette industry's activities was, up to this time, self-imposed, especially in the area of advertising. The early 1920s were char-acterized by an industry understanding that women were not to be shown in advertisements. Liggett and Myers, who produced Chester-

FIGURE 1
Per Capita Consumption of Various Tobacco Products, 1900-1948

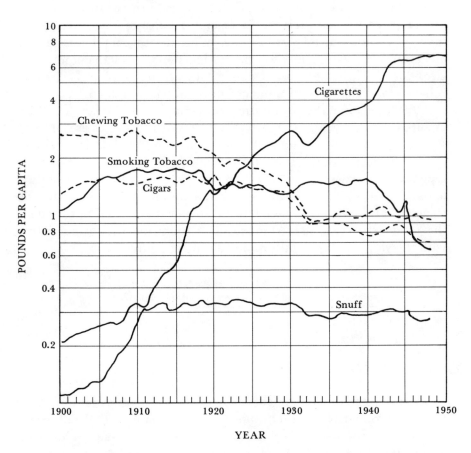

Source: Richard B. Tennant, *The American Tobacco Industry* (New Haven:
          Yale University Press, 1950), 127.

field, were the first to undermine this understanding,[13] and the
other companies followed suit. This inability to maintain a joint
voluntary understanding among firms in the cigarette industry, a
weakness which was underscored in later years, is a common phenomenon in industries structured as oligopolies.

In other areas of the industry's activities, however, explicit
collusion is evident. The first and the most obvious case of such

collusion was evidenced by the market practices of the American Tobacco Company between the years 1890 and 1911. The company was formed in 1890 by consolidating five manufacturing companies which controlled ninety percent of cigarette production (then a minor segment of total tobacco production) and less than ten percent of other tobacco products. By 1910, the American Tobacco Company had acquired monopolistic control of every branch of the industry except cigars. Furthermore, by creating a new corporation with the British Imperial Tobacco Company — the British-American company in which Americans controlled two-thirds of the interests — they were able to construct what amounted to a monopoly over foreign markets as well.[14] Such activities did not go without notice, and on May 11, 1911, the Supreme Court found the American Tobacco Company (better known as the Tobacco Trust) guilty of violating the Sherman Act.[15]

The Court, following the precedent set a few years earlier in the antitrust case against Standard Oil, designed a dissolution plan which was implemented a few months later. The plan broke the trust into fourteen different companies. From these, four emerged with significant economic potential. These were the American Tobacco Company, Liggett and Myers, P. Lorillard, and R. J. Reynolds. By the early 1920s the "big four" controlled ninety-two percent of the cigarette market.[16]

The verdict against the trust and the decision to dissolve it are compatible with an attempt to maintain freedom of exchange in the market, a function which economic "minimalists" reserved for the government.[17] However, the implementation of the dissolution plan was not entirely successful. For example, Judge Brandeis launched the following criticism:

> The decision was wholly unsatisfactory. Under the plan approved by the Court the Tobacco Company will be in a better position than it was before the government brought suit against it under the Sherman Law, because it can do in the future, under the legal sanction of the decree, things that had heretofore been considered in violation of the law.[18]

Brandeis was correct regarding at least one aspect of the industry's activity, that of pricing. On two occasions, in 1944 and 1946, the big four were found guilty of monopolization, and specifically of conducting non-competitive price practices.[19] To understand what led to such a decision requires us to go one step backward.

After the dissolution of the Tobacco Trust, R. J. Reynolds, a small company at that time, experienced overwhelming success with its Camel brand. A combination of effective advertising and Turkish taste helped turn Camel into the leading brand for almost two decades. The other firms responded by offering similar brands and by concentrating their advertising almost entirely on a single brand. Thus, American came out with Lucky Strike, while Liggett and Myers offered Chesterfield. Each of the brands was designed to appeal to some segment of the population that was not reached by the other brands. In 1925 the three aforementioned brands constituted eighty-two percent of the domestic market. The delayed, and therefore relatively modest, success of Lorillard with Old Gold brought the combined market share of the big four with regard to these four brands to about ninety-two percent by the end of the 1920s.

Only two companies successfully penetrated the market during the 1930s, namely Philip Morris and Brown and Williamson. This may be attributed to the fact that during the Depression they sold "economy brands" which cost five cents less per package than the standard brands offered by the big four. The increase in the standard of living after the Depression and toward the end of the 1930s put an end to the inexpensive economy brands. By that time, however, the two companies had already established their market position and were able to market popular standard brands of their own. The structure of the cigarette industry today reflects this historical process. It is an oligopolistic industry comprised of six large firms, trailed by a few very small ones.[20] The big six control ninety-nine percent of the market.

Table A shows a comparison of list prices among the six leading brands of the big six between 1935 and 1950. The table appears to demonstrate price collusion. Where price differentials do exist, it is only a matter of a few cents, and on the retail level these differences were "rounded up." [21] The only exception, until 1940, was Philip Morris. A pattern developed, and continues to exist; when one firm announced a price change, the others responded immediately by adjusting their prices. Alternatively, those firms instigating the price increase were forced to roll back prices, as in the case of American in December 1941 and Liggett and Myers in August 1946. Thus, consumers are faced with only one market price. "The high concentration and the infrequency of price changes in the cigarette industry are facts beyond dispute," writes Lester Telser; "hence the theory of perfect competition is of little help in explaining the behavior of cigarette companies."[22]

The theory of perfect competition predicts that all firms in the industry will charge the same price for a given product. However, the observed price rigidity is incompatible with this theory, given that yearly fluctuations in the price of tobacco leaves and other manufacturing costs do not appear to affect prices as they should. In the next chapter we shall elaborate on this.

TABLE A.　Manufacturers' List Prices of Six Leading Standard Brands, 1935-1950
(in dollars per thousand cigarettes)

Effective date of price change	Camel (Reynolds)	Lucky Strike (American)	Chesterfield (Liggett & Myers)	Old Gold (Lorillard)	Raleigh (B&W)	Philip Morris (Philip Morris)
9-2-35	6.10	6.10	6.10	6.10	6.10	6.85
1-19-37	6.25*	6.10	6.25	6.10	6.10	6.85
1-20-37	6.25	6.25	6.25	6.25	6.10	6.85
7-15-37	6.25	6.25	6.25	6.25	6.25	6.85
7-1-40	6.53*	6.53	6.53	6.53	6.53	6.85
Unknown	6.53	6.53	6.53	6.53	6.53	6.53
12-28-41	6.53	7.10*	6.53	6.53	6.53	6.53
12-30-41	6.53	6.53	6.53	6.53	6.53	6.53
11-1-42	6.81	6.81	6.81	6.81	6.81	6.81
4-25-46	7.09	7.09	7.09	7.09	7.09	7.09
8-1-46	7.09	7.09	7.31*	7.09	7.09	7.09
8-5-46	7.09	7.09	7.09	7.09	7.09	7.09
10-8-46	7.09	7.38*	7.09	7.09	7.09	7.38
10-10-46	7.09	7.38	7.38	7.38	7.09	7.38
10-14-46	7.35	7.38	7.38	7.38	7.09	7.38
Unknown	7.35	7.38	7.38	7.38	7.38	7.38
7-28-48	7.35	7.78*	7.38	7.38	7.38	7.79
7-29-48	7.75	7.78	7.38	7.38	7.38	7.79
7-30-48	7.75	7.78	7.78	7.78	7.78	7.79
5-?-49	7.78	7.78	7.78	7.78	7.78	7.79
7-26-50	8.00*	7.78	7.78	7.78	7.78	7.79
7-28-50	8.00	8.00	8.00	8.00	8.00	8.00

* First firm to announce change in prices

Source: William H. Nicholls, *Price Policies in the Cigarette Industry* (Nashville: Vanderbilt University Press, 1951), pp. 116, 152.

Accepting the proposition that there is no price competition in the cigarette industry does not mean that firms do not compete with each other. On the contrary, cigarette firms often behave aggressively toward each other in the market arena. The rivalry is usually manifested in advertising. It was this domain that the government decided to regulate during the 1960s.

THE PUBLIC GOOD PERIOD

Several events led the government to intervene in the activities of the tobacco industry during the 1960s. Some actions were rooted in reports which appeared during the 1950s linking cigarette smoking to lung cancer and other diseases. The first warning notes connecting smoking with health were sounded in 1939 by Dr. Alton Ochsner, a surgeon (later to become president of the American Cancer Society), and then again in the late 1940s by Dr. Ernst Synder. "Those findings created hardly a ripple in the medical circles and even less in the public circles."[23] In 1951, similar findings by two English physicians, Dr. Richard Doll and Dr. A. B. Hill, were aired by the mass media and thereby became part of public awareness. Perhaps this signalled the beginning of the trend toward public intervention that peaked a decade later.

It is commonly believed that publication of these findings contributed to the drop of about 6.5 percent in the level of cigarette consumption between the years 1952 and 1954. However, at least one authority on the cigarette industry, Harry M. Wootten, has expressed the opinion that the "health scare" was only one factor that contributed to this decline and that there were several other factors that may have had greater impact on consumers. Among them he mentions:[24]

1. Decline in new smokers as a result of a lower birth rate during the Depression.
2. Mounting tax surcharges (federal, state and municipal) on each package.
3. Drop in personal income.
4. Rise in king-size sales (i.e., the sale of fewer units for the same amount of tobacco, thus reducing the units smoked).

The fourth point is of some interest and deserves further explanation.

Between 1952 and 1954 there was an increase of about ten percent (from 18.3 percent to 28.1 percent) in the consumption of non-filter king-size cigarettes. These cigarette types contain about twenty percent more tobacco per unit than the non-filter standard brands. Hence people bought fewer units but received the same "satisfaction." By 1976 the market share of non-filter king-size cigarettes was less than seven percent. Thus, the declining position of these cigarettes helped restore consumption to previous levels. On the other hand, a combination of health warnings, which presumably made some people aware of the risk involved in smoking, and the industry's response, in the form of promoting "safer" filter cigarettes, helped change the pattern of consumption. More and more smokers switched to those cigarettes. The filter brands, which are currently most successful, had been introduced by that time. Philip Morris marketed an unsuccessful plain cigarette and turned it into the presently most successful filter brand, Marlboro. R. J. Reynolds introduced two winners by the mid 1950s — Winston and later Salem. By that time, Brown and Williamson's factories could not meet the demand for Viceroy. Tareyton (American), Kent (P. Lorillard), and L & M (Liggett and Myers) were other successful filter introductions (see Appendix B).

The combined effect of all this was to increase the market position of the filter brands from 1.4 percent in 1952 to almost ninety percent in 1976. The position of plain standard cigarettes declined during that period from 80.3 percent to a mere 3.4 percent, and it is still declining.

Now consider the following:

the filter tip enables the manufacturer to produce a cigarette with a smaller tobacco content while maintaining overall dimensions and avoiding waste of tobacco in the unsmoked fag-end.[25]

In addition, filters use cheaper grades of tobacco leaf, which have a stronger taste, so that the smoker will get more flavor despite the filter. The manufacturers use more of the tobacco leaf because of better machinery. "Ultimately, fifteen percent less tobacco is used for an average cigarette than was needed a decade ago."[26] It seems then, that the unit-per-pound argument worked in favor of the industry after the mid 1950s, while previously it worked against the industry.

Two incidents of intervention were logged in the 1950s. On September 15, 1955, and on December 17, 1959, the Federal Trade Commission intervened in the activities of the industry by promulgating a cigarette advertising guide which prohibited any health claims, direct or indirect, with regard to tobacco products.

The serious problems faced by the industry in the 1960s began in March 1962 with the publication by the Royal College of Physicians in London of a report entitled *Smoking and Health.* Consequently, the Italian government banned all cigarette advertising. (In Great Britain cigarette advertising on television was banned in 1965.) The American public took note of these developments, and in June 1962 the Surgeon General, Dr. Luther L. Terry, announced, with President Kennedy's approval, the formation of the Advisory Committee on Smoking and Health.[27] In November of that year, a federal district court jury ruled in a test case that Liggett and Myers' Chesterfield had been "one of the causes" of lung cancer in a Pittsburgh carpenter. The jury did not find the company liable, holding that the smoker had knowingly assumed the risk of injury by his heavy smoking. Nevertheless, the health-and-smoking connection had become more salient than the industry cared for.[28] Other cases followed, and the industry employed a battery of defense lawyers for personal injury suits.[29]

On January 11, 1964, the advisory committee released its report. The document, which became known as the *Surgeon General's Report,* contained two major conclusions:

Cigarette smoking is a health hazard of sufficient importance in the United States to warrant remedial action.

Cigarette smoking is causally related to lung cancer in men; the magnitude of the effect of cigarette smoking far outweighs other factors. The data for women, although less extensive, point in the same direction.[30]

The report caused a decline in total consumption for that year of about two percent. But more important, within a week, on January 18, the FTC announced initiation of proceedings for "promulgation of trade regulation rules regarding unfair and deceptive acts or practices in the advertising and labelling of cigarettes."[31] In the summer of the same year, while the House of Representatives committee held hearings on the smoking-and-health issue, the FTC issued (June 22) a ruling requiring all cigarette advertising and packages to display the notice: "Cigarette smoking is *dangerous* to health and may cause *death* from cancer and other diseases" (emphasis added).[32] When Congress completed the hearings a year later, it designed and enacted the Cigarette Labelling and Advertising Act. The act, signed by President Johnson, required a health warning to be printed on cigarette packages. The text of the warning was as follows: "Cigarette smoking may be *hazardous* to your health" (emphasis added).[33] It is striking how mild the latter text is as compared with the FTC version.

The act also included a provision which for three years prevented any federal, state, or local authority from requiring that cigarette advertising include a statement relating to smoking and health. In addition, the FTC was required to wait five years, until the expiration of the act, before proposing new advertising requirements. It is not difficult to see that the negative effects on the industry were minimal. In fact, as stated by Elizabeth Drew, the label might even be a boon of sorts, providing new defense for the industry in further personal injury cases brought by cigarette smokers.[34] Two close observers of the legislative process that led to the bill arrived at basically the same conclusion. Drew even entitled her article "The Quiet Victory of the Cigarette Lobby: How it Found the Best Filter Yet — Congress." Fritschler suggested that the bill was "more a victory for cigarettes than it was for health."[35] Thus, in 1965, cigarette consumption rose about 3.5 percent, passing 1963's total by about seven billion units.

Nonetheless, from the standpoint of the health groups involved, the bill, mild as it was, represented a victory inasmuch as the government had finally committed itself to an official position in declaring smoking to be harmful to health. Some measures, however limited, had been undertaken by the government against the industry.[36] The long-term effect was to legitimize the smoking issue as an object for vigorous public policy experimentation and public debate. The issue was brought to the forefront of the congressional agenda and stayed there for years to come. This could not help but bring the political activities of the cigarette industry and their opponents into the public arena. Thus, while the first health warnings in 1939 and in the early 1950s generated only a negligible governmental response, between 1964 and 1966 the issue became an important topic for debate by public and regulatory commissions.

While the FTC continued its traditional role as a watchdog over the market practices of the cigarette firms, with the increased attention to the product itself, it was the Federal Communications Commission, now broadened, which prevented the industry from enjoying the fruits of victory for long.

In 1967, a combined effort on the part of New York attorney John F. Banzhaf III and the FCC resulted in a regulation of unprecedented scope in the realm of government intervention in the activities of this industry, the Fairness Doctrine. Previously this regulation had been applied only to political issues. It reflected the duty of radio and television licensees to "operate in the public interest and to afford reasonable opportunity for the discussion of conflicting views on issues of public importance."[37] It seems that here the tobacco industry was caught off guard. They left much of the action in the courts to the National Association of Broadcasters, who of course would stand to lose substantial revenue if forced to allocate free broadcasting time to health groups. Lydon estimated that between 1968 and 1970, when the Fairness Doctrine was implemented with respect to cigarette advertising, the health groups received seventy-five million dollars' worth of broadcast time each year.[38] The doctrine required that the opposing view be reasonably represented and, as a measure of balance, that the ratio of cigarette commercials to antismoking commercials be set at three to one.[39] In order to monitor the effective maintenance of that ratio, Mr. Banzhaf formed ASH (Action on Smoking and Health) in February 1968. On June 12 of that year, ASH filed the first of many petitions demanding that the license of various stations be revoked due to failure to devote sufficient air time to antismoking messages.

The next stage in the "war against smoking" was the action taken by the two regulatory commissions, the FCC and the FTC. They pressured Congress to ban all cigarette advertising from television and radio. The commissions were following strategies used in eleven other countries including Great Britain (1965), Italy (1962), Norway, Sweden, Switzerland, the Soviet Union, and Poland, where prohibitions on cigarette advertising had already been effected.[40]

On February 5, 1969, the FCC issued notice of a proposed ruling to ban the broadcast of cigarette advertising because "the presentation of commercials promoting the use of cigarettes is inconsistent with the obligation imposed upon broadcasters to operate in the public interest."[41] On their part, the FTC, now freed from the restriction imposed by the 1965 Cigarette Labelling Act, released a statement to the Senate Committee on Cigarette Labelling on July 22, 1969. This offered to suspend the dread regulation ruling until July 1971, if the tobacco industry would take cigarette advertising off the air voluntarily or if such advertising were banned by legislative action.[42] The result was the Public Health Cigarette Smoking Act of 1969, which was signed by President Nixon on April 1, 1970.[43] Paragraph B of the act prohibited the advertising of cigarettes on broadcast media after January 1, 1971.

The ban was hailed by the antismoking forces as a major victory. They did not foresee one serious drawback — since the broadcasters could no longer advertise cigarettes, they were no longer required to comply with the Fairness Doctrine. Consequently, the frequency of

TABLE B. Number of Antismoking Messages Delivered by
the American Lung Association, 1969-1974

Year	Total Number of Network Spots	
	Television	*Radio*
Pre-ban		
1969	647	—
1970	622	—
Post-ban		
1971	116	99
1972	127	95
1973	231	98
1974	95*	336*

*Only two of the three networks reported.

antismoking spots was reduced and they were aired at night instead of during prime time. The influence of the controversy on the public was dampened, and cigarette consumption rose significantly. The figures in Table B represent partial information concerning the frequency of the antismoking spots aired by only one member of the health coalition, the American Lung Association.[44]

The health forces neglected to observe what really happened to cigarette consumption in any of the countries from which they drew their inspiration. In Britain, for example, the 1965 ban did not reduce the level of cigarette consumption. On the other hand, the imposition of the Fairness Doctrine in the United States did have the effect of depressing consumption. Logic dictates that if A exists because of B, then if B is removed A will cease to exist. Even Elizabeth Drew, whose analysis of the 1965 act was so astute, failed to realize this simple logic. In the May 4, 1969, *New York Times Magazine,* she wrote an article entitled "The Cigarette Companies Would Rather Fight Than Switch". Others, however, did not overlook the obvious. Professor John Mueller of Rochester, disturbed by the article, wrote a letter to the editor which accurately predicted the post-ban developments and captured the essence of the dilemma.

May 5, 1969

To the Editor:

There are a couple of observations in the article on smoking by Elizabeth H. Drew in the May 4 issue which seem to lead to a disturbing conclusion.

She suggests, first, that television antismoking ads apparently have been influential in decreasing the incidence of smoking. Second, she states that bans on TV cigarette ads in other countries have not been effective in reducing smoking.

But, if the FCC is successful in banning cigarette commercials in this country, television stations apparently would no longer be required to present the antismoking messages as they are now under the "fairness" doctrine.

The net effect of the ban, therefore, might well be to maintain cigarette consumption at a higher level than would prevail without the ban.

With enemies like the FCC, the tobacco industry hardly needs friends.

Sincerely,

John E. Mueller

The letter, unfortunately, was not printed.

In the following chapters it is suggested that long before May 1969, the industry was aware of exactly what the repercussions of the ban would be. Furthermore, it is posited that it was in their own self-interest, as profit maximizers, to withdraw broadcast advertisements.

Although the two regulatory commissions continued their intervention into the activities of the cigarette industry after 1971, there has been nothing of major significance (see Appendix A).

SUMMARY

Two phases have been recognized and outlined in the public attitude toward the cigarette industry and its product during the present century.

The private good period lasted from the beginning of the century until the early 1960s. Although the product was considered "evil" by some groups, it was generally accepted as a normal consumer item. The public regulated the activities of the industry, not because of the product itself, but rather because of unacceptable practices of manufacturing and marketing, such as monopolistic behavior and noncompetitive market practices.

The public good period began in the 1960s and continues to the present. In this period regulatory actions against the industry have been implemented because the "public interest" was to be protected. The sanctions were therefore against the product itself.

Perhaps the acts effected by the government in the second period have had the same economic implications as they would have if undertaken during the first period. The difference lies in the norms, the theory, and the justification of the intervention. In the first period, the government guarded the public's material well-being against economic misconduct and exploitation. In the second, especially after the Surgeon General's report, the government tried to protect the public's physical well-being by regulating information about the product.

The second period can be seen as inherently different from the first from another perspective. Certainly the attitude toward smoking had changed, but more important, certain governmental units

had become engaged in attempting to make the issue part of the
federal agenda. Once an item is on the agenda, writes Kenneth
Arrow,

> . . . it is difficult not to treat it in a somewhat rational manner,
> if this is at all possible . . . [and since] there are some problems
> for which there are no satisfactory solutions, placing such an
> item on the agenda may create a demand for a solution which
> will of necessity be unsatisfactory.[45]

The government solution was regulation, and in the following
chapters we will show that from the public point of view it was
unsatisfactory.

THREE

The Political Regulation of an Industry

THREE

The theoretical discussion advanced in this chapter will be divided into two parts: a general presentation of the nature and dynamics of public regulation and an analysis of competition among firms in a regulated oligopolistic market. The analysis implicitly assumes a dynamic "regulatory space" which varies with and expands over time. Thus, in comparison to the beginning of the century, this space is much larger today. The nature of the distribution of costs and benefits from various regulations among the members of society serves as an aid in the conceptualization of this space. More specifically, the space can be defined along two dimensions where the benefits (costs) from (of) various regulations are either concentrated or diffused among the many members of society.

To illustrate: A situation characterized by concentrated costs and benefits typifies those regulations which involve two industries engaged in conflict; a situation defined by diffused costs and benefits deals with the common type of regulation such as income taxes or traffic regulations; a situation where the costs are concentrated and benefits are diffused is less common and pertains to cases where, for example, restrictions are imposed only on certain groups (a case in point is the situation of blacks in the South prior to 1950); finally, in situations where concentrated benefits and diffused costs prevail, an industry benefits while the public bears the costs of the regulation. The regulation of the cigarette industry serves as a case study for this last kind of situation.

To begin with, drawing on examples from the entire regulatory space, the chapter argues that for industries, public regulation is an available political solution to economic problems. Second, we establish that in fact the industry, because of its particular market situation, may be motivated to acquire such regulation. Further, it is shown that being "forced" to acquire a political solution to its economic problems is not necessarily incompatible with the industry goal of profit maximization.

PUBLIC REGULATION – DEFINITION

Regulation in the broadest sense is a requirement, imposed by self or others, on an individual or group, not to perform an activity that would be undertaken in the absence of such restraint. The regulation becomes a framework, of sorts, activated in the present with the purpose of establishing the scope, the ground rules, and the context in which decisions should take place in the future.

The reasons for restricting an individual or group from choosing a particular mode of behavior and the mechanisms employed in this restriction may vary from one social context to another. It may result from one person's decision to regulate others, as in a dictatorial situation. Or a majority of individuals or their representatives may vote to do so, as in the case of Congress or in a federal commission. Individual behavior may also be regulated by some kind of impersonal mechanism – the price system in a market economy is such a device, as is a moral code, dictated presumably by "extra-human" forces.

In most cases, when our range of alternatives is being limited by others, it is because one or many individuals in society inflict externalities on other members of society and thus on society at large. The purpose of public regulation is to restrict the range of these individuals' available alternative actions in such a way that they will have to alter or modify their behavior and consequently will not impose the external effects on others (at least, not in the same manner) as they did prior to the restriction. After the regulation, if people do not change their pattern of behavior, or if the outcome after the regulatory act is similar to what happened prior to it, then either the public act was ineffective or, for whatever reason, the public is unable to prevent a minority from undertaking an "undesired" action.

Any kind of regulatory proposal should involve a calculation of the costs and benefits which society anticipates will evolve from the proposed change. Essential in this calculation are the costs of implementation, supervision, and enforcement. When we deal with a mass phenomenon, rooted in the population, the cost of enforcement may be so high as to render methods of regulation a priori ineffective. A classic example of such an attempt to regulate behavior is the prohibition of alcohol.[1]

REGULATORY POLICIES –
A POLITICAL RESOLUTION OF CONFLICT

When society "decides" to regulate some future alternative act of a member, or group of members, such a decision is political by definition.[2] One essential element of politics is conflict. A conflictive situation occurs when two or more parties (individuals, groups) have opposing interests or claims over the same space or time. The outcome of a conflict is related, of course, to the objectives and the means used by the particular parties engaged. In addition, it is dependent on their resources and the effort invested to achieve a solution. A solution may simply take the form of an agreement, a "social contract" of sorts, or it may be an explicit law. "The function of a given law is usually to prevent conflict, to resolve conflict, or to constrain conflict within agreed upon limits."[3]

The regulatory act, or law, as a solution may thus vary in its degree of comprehensiveness, according to the nature of the conflict. The public may decide, for example, to install traffic lights on road intersections in order to prevent potential conflict among drivers. The benefits are clear – prevention of potential accidents. The cost involves such elements as installation, electricity, and the loss of time to the motorists who must wait when the light is red. The public may decide that such regulatory apparatus is too costly, so that the rule "the first vehicle to enter an intersection shall have the right of way" will suffice. However, the first alternative may become more attractive if the level of conflict – in this case, the number of automobile accidents – increases.

When dealing with the public regulation of an industry, we must recognize that a conflictual situation is inherent in each act. In different times, on different occasions, and across different industries, a firm may be in conflict with others over actual or potential customers, over entering or maintaining status in the market, over competing firms providing complementary or substitutionary goods and services, over individuals or groups opposing one or another aspect of the firm's activities, and so on. In many of these situations the government is not called on. The rival parties may arrive at a solution themselves. "In order to end the conflict," writes Coser,

the parties must agree upon rules and norms allowing them to assess the respective power positions in the struggle. Their common interest leads them to accept rules which enhance their mutual dependence in the very pursuit of their antagonistic goals.[4]

Thus, in a market situation where a seller and a buyer are involved, the price system regulates the conflict. If they do not agree on a given price, the transaction does not occur, even though the seller wants to sell and the buyer wants to buy.

In such cases the government is called on only in the initial stage, to set up the ground rules for the economic activity. When all parties agree on and act in accordance with the ground rules, the extent of government involvement in the market becomes minimal. By imposing boundaries, therefore, the government does not necessarily have to get involved in the actual conflict. The Sherman Act, for example, prohibits monopolization of the market by one firm. Thus it proposes to guarantee free and fair competition among firms in the industry. This is also supposed to generate reasonable price levels for the consumer.

As long as the firms in the industry follow the rules of antitrust legislation, there is no need for governmental intervention. The government, with its court system, will be called on only if a firm attempts to monopolize the market.[5]

Clearly there are times, perhaps many times, when the government becomes a partner in a conflict. In some cases this partnership is a permanent one. For example, when the government regulates the retail price level of an industry, its supervision must be constant to assure that no violations occur. Often it is necessary for it to establish a normative justification in order not to render the act artibrary. The public official, aware of this necessity, generally finds justification by appealing to the "public interest."

> The "public interest" is the standard that guides the administrator in executing the law . . . this concept is to the bureaucracy what the "due process" clause is to the judiciary.[6]

When regulations are imposed at an economic level, they may and often do produce counterproductive results. The adverse outcomes resulting from rent control, minimum wage and zoning regulations are examples which come to mind.[7] Furthermore, the government is often seen as investing enormous energy in order to produce only questionable results. While one governmental organ is fighting the undesirable by-products of an industry, another organ may be subsidizing the industry, enabling them to continue producing the undesirable product. This situation is true in the case of the cigarette industry. While the Department of Health, Education and Welfare and the regulatory agencies are fighting smoking, the Department of Agriculture subsidizes tobacco growers, thus helping to maintain the price of tobacco.[8] This apparent inconsistency is not surprising, particularly in a decentralized federal government such as exists in the United States. It can be explained partly by the absence of a comprehensive coordinating body and partly by the multi-dimensionality of the concept of "public interest" or, as the economist would like to call it, "public welfare."

Governments exist and function, presumably, in order to serve society and help increase its welfare. The government is organized in such a way that several units are placed in charge of different components of this general goal of aiding the public welfare. As each unit attempts to maximize the efficient implementation of a particular sub-goal, the various units often find themselves in opposition to each other.[9] Decisions to increase, for example, the level of employment, to achieve a stable economy, or to balance the budget may be inconsistent with decisions to protect the environment, improve health conditions, reduce inflation, and so on. The situation was probably best described by Emmette Redford, who wrote:

> We cannot expect a full measure of consistency in public policy. In a dynamic, free, pluralistic society the balance of forces which play upon government and which interact within it is constantly shifting. Within government, moves made contemporaneously at different points may not be synchronized — may even have conflicting effects — and moves made over a period of time may reflect great changes in purposes and effects. The process of administrative and political decision are sensitive in too many directions for men to hope or to fear for a congruency of policies . . . the realized public interest in a free society is no neat package of consistent elements.[10]

Inconsistencies in the realized public interest, which are especially manifest in a free and democratic society, are also the consequence of the absence of a satisfactory method for aggregating individual preferences that will perfectly reflect the desires of the people.[11]

The various governmental organs, in order to better their interests and those of their clients, compete between themselves for control of public policies.[12] In this competition a process of coalition formation often emerges. Initiation of this process need not come from the government; it can come from the industry which may form a coalition with one governmental agency whose goals oppose those of another coalition — one which includes a different governmental unit. The mere inclusion of the government changes the nature of the conflict from an economic one to a political one or to a mixture of the two.[13] Short of a voluntary agreement, government is the only legitimate body that can impose regulatory acts on the other members of the coalition or on the citizenry at large.

The regulatory act, a sort of political solution, may often be preferred by a particular interest group to the economic solution of the market. In fact, a political solution may often be the only way to save an industry from economic disaster. This is because in the political arena, where power plays an important role, it is often easier to combat the opposition successfully. The reason is, simply, that in politics rivals must articulate their positions and their demands. Hence, it becomes easier to identify them and to make an approximation of their relative power base.

The readiness of a group to work toward the acquisition of a solution to a conflict depends on its resources and on its assessment of the opposition's readiness to channel resources into the conflict. The achievement of a solution close to its own preferred goal constitutes the benefit to be gained, while the resources invested in order to achieve these benefits constitute the cost. It would be surprising to discover, writes Stigler, "that for a given regulatory policy, a group with larger benefits and low cost of political action [was] being dominated by another group with lesser benefits and higher cost of political action."[14] This is not to say that the less powerful group has no impact on the policy process and its outcomes. On the contrary, Lindblom's observation that all affected interests can have at least some influence in the policy-making process is valid.[15] Their power does not lie in the ability to affect the outcome, but rather the outcome (the act) is designed with consideration of the position or objective of the other side. Thus, the regulatory act, even when it is "acquired by the industry and is designed and operated primarily for its benefit" is not independent of the nature of the opposition.[16] If the opposition, the weaker coalition, can regroup in the future, it may effect a new design of an act.

The political process of regulation, as recognized here, is dynamic in nature. At different points in time, the circumstances of the intensity and duration of the conflict, and the stakes involved, will vary. The conflict may often be characterized as a zero-sum situation, in which the gain of a favorable regulation by one side is considered a direct loss to the other side. In other conflictual episodes, the rivals may arrive at some compromise, agreeing on a solution that will benefit them both, i.e., a non-zero-sum situation. For example, the decision to ban advertising of cigarettes from the broadcasting media was *perceived* by the public as a major victory to the health coalition and as a severe loss to the tobacco industry.

On the other hand, the decision to impose a requirement demanding information regarding the level of tar and nicotine contained in each cigarette in advertisements in the print media cannot be considered a victory to the health coalition but rather should be considered a compromise. Such a requirement seems to benefit both sides. First, the health coalition and the industry were interested (each from its own perspective) in shifting consumer taste toward low tar and nicotine cigarettes. The provision of such information was, among other things, an important factor in stimulating this shift. Second, the determination of the content of tar and nicotine has been undertaken by the FTC, which utilizes its own laboratories for this purpose. The cost of gathering the information is thus not internalized by the firms in the industry, although they make use of this information in their advertisements.

The regulatory process is continued over time; thus when one side loses even a crucial regulatory decision it may still be able to generate opposition in the future. Public organizations will usually continue to function even though they might have lost a regulatory battle. Concerned members of a losing coalition may regroup their

ranks, add or subtract (if possible) members, and attempt once again
to achieve the desired outcome or an improved compromise. For
some regulated industries, because of the time element involved,
the process may exhibit a feature of co-optation.[17] That is, because
of continued engagement and common and specialized knowledge
concerning the issues involved, good relationships and perhaps even
shared values may emerge between one coalition (the regulators)
and the other coalition (the regulated industry). This may lead to a
situation where the interest of the regulators coincides with the
interest of the regulated. Consequently, some observers of the regulatory process have suggested that the regulators tend to be "captured" by the regulated.[18] Utility industries are, of course, the
example cited most often. People with such diverse opinions as
those of Milton Friedman and consumer advocate Ralph Nader have
in fact argued that regulators are almost certain to be dominated
by the industry they are supposed to regulate.[19] Others have argued
that, on the contrary, the industry is captured by the regulators:
"since the business of an agency is to regulate, [thus], they pro-
claim policies which are designed to keep them in business."[20]

Whether or not one accepts either of these positions is of secondary importance. The important point is the realization that in virtually every major American industry there is an attempt to impose
some sort of regulation. Hence the conflict cuts across major parts of
the domestic economic and political space. It should also be realized
that in most cases the regulatory process exhibits a mixture of
community interests and antagonistic interests between the sides
involved in the conflict. The regulatory outcome may favor, or
at least will be perceived as favoring, one side over another. It is not
always a clear zero-sum situation, nor is it always in each and every
episode of interaction a cooperative situation.

Understanding the regulatory process as a dynamic one implies
that over time, regulation with regard to a given industry may be
the outcome of conflict among coalitions which are not necessarily
identical each time. These coalitions will be formed anew in different conflictual contexts. On this, Cyert and March remark as
follows:

. . . drawing the boundaries of an organizational coalition once
and for all is impossible. Instead we simplify the conception by
focusing on the participant in a particular "region" — either
temporal or functional. That is, over a specified (relatively
brief) period of time we can identify the major coalition members; or for a particular decision we can identify the major
coalition members.[21]

The nature of the coalition — its intensity, its members, the extent
to which it is ready to invest in acquiring a solution, and so on,
will determine the outcome. Since the context of conflict may
differ from one point in time to another, it is likely that a given
industry will win some conflicts and lose others.

Given this changing nature of the coalition, is it possible to
determine when an act will favor the industry? According to Stigler
and Wilson the answer appears to rest in the understanding of the
costs and benefits of a given regulatory act.[22] In particular, we can
expect that when the benefits are concentrated within the industry
and when the costs generated by the act are diffused among many
members of society, the act will tend to favor the industry. But the
identification of relevant costs and benefits is not an easy task.
One can, however, approach this question indirectly, utilizing Riker's
coalitions theory.[23]

It is assumed that a "firm" is a profit maximizer and that it
will be risk averse when faced with a threat.[24] When an external
source seriously threatens the profit margin or even the existence of
the firm and the industry, one would expect the industry to form a
"grand coalition" or "coalition of the whole." Grand coalitions
occur when the "small game (i.e., among, for example, firms in the
marketplace) is embedded in a larger one, the players in the smaller
game may form a coalition of the whole in the smaller game in order
to win in the larger one."[25] In the case of cigarettes, the industry
formed a coalition of the whole in order to combat politically the
antismoking forces. Arend Lijphart and Eric Nordlinger, in their
respective studies on political conflict, also describe this tendency,
concluding that in time of crisis, the opposing parties in a system

tend to ignore their differences and engage in a joint effort to combat the source of the threat.[26]

Grand coalitions, of course, are not allowed to form for economic purposes at the market level (due to regulation which prohibits
collusive acts), but they are permitted at the political level. On the
other hand, the source creating the threat presumably also needs
to form a coalition in order to be an "equal" match for the industry.
When two industries are in conflict, the stronger, as Stigler suggested, will dominate the weaker. But when the industry faces a
non-market group, "fighting in the name of the public," the situation is quite different.

> Organizations purporting to speak for very large sectors (e.g.,
> the public) are often active in regulatory politics, but in many
> cases the positions they take are either highly general (so as to
> avoid antagonizing any element of diverse membership) or
> unrepresentative because they are responsive to the interests
> and beliefs of an activist minority rather than to those of a broad
> constituency.[27]

Either way, the coalition formed by the industry finds itself
in an advantageous situation. The industry has been forced to clarify
its goals, and motivation has been intensified, not simply because
the stakes seem to be higher, but also, as Olson suggested, because of
their sheer size.[28] The coalition will thus usually win a favorable
regulation when the threat is sufficiently serious. The more econom-
ically prominent the industry, the better it may fare in the regulatory arena. The gains for the industry should be understood in
terms of their economic meaning. Often, the gains are not easily
recognized and may indeed materialize only over time.

To summarize this section: The public regulation of a given industry is perceived as a process rather than as a single act. The process is political in essence and involves political coalitions, loosely
defined, engaged in a conflictual situation. The regulatory act is
a political solution to such conflict, and the solution will tend to
favor industry over non-industry interests.

The next section of this chapter will demonstrate that the
regulatory process may often create a situation in which one regulation may breed another regulation which can nullify the first.

PUBLIC REGULATION OF OLIGOPOLISTIC INDUSTRY

This section moves away from the general discussion of public regulation to a theoretical analysis of such regulation with regard to oligopolistic industry. The discussion is divided into two parts. Both are concerned with the nature of the product the industry manufactures. The first part (Market Situation A) is concerned with a product which is primarily considered to be a private good. It is being produced by an industry structured as an oligopoly, where the firms compete among themselves for consumers by means of advertising. The second part (Market Situation B) deals with a public good, in the sense previously defined of a product which is considered to produce externalities on the public when consumed.[29] The controversy over the product's externalities, and the subsequent introduction of this issue on the government agenda, breeds market uncertainty which was not present before. This may lead to regulations which are compatible with the industry's interests. Although the discussion is generalized, we have utilized, when necessary, examples from the cigarette industry.

Market Situation A

A private good is one that does not produce externalities, or deleterious consequences, while being consumed. In order to continually produce such an item, a firm must find or create a market for it. People will buy the product only if they prefer having it over not having it. Their actual purchase of the product depends on budget, time, and mobility constraints. They will buy it if in their preference ordering they rank that product higher than other products. By buying product A, an individual also makes a decision not to buy product B. When he decides to buy product A he may be faced with several brands which satisfy his definition of product A. His decision to buy brand X and not Y or Z is affected, of course, by the relative price of the brands and the other attributes that may be assigned to different brands, i.e., attractiveness of packing, familiarity with the product, experience with and trust in the consistency and level of quality of the product, and so on. His continued decision to purchase a given brand in future visits to the market — his loyalty to the brand — depends largely on the satisfaction derived from consuming the product in the past. If he is satisfied with the brand, if the anticipated attributes assigned to the product materialize, he will tend to be loyal to the product. Note, however, that an explanation as to why the "shopper" bought the product in the first place is not provided. It is suggested that he bought it because he preferred having it. Different people may buy the same product for different reasons. The reasons may be psychological desires, imitation, physical needs, socialization, and so on.

In the absence of precise knowledge as to why people behave the way they do, firms in the industry compete among themselves in order to provide products that will satisfy the demand of various consumers. This competition involves offering better prices, quality, services, information, and so on. The firms design their marketing strategies in such a way as to enable them to increase their sales and hence their profit.[30]

Although the firm is commonly assumed to be a profit maximizer, we must realize that making a profit for the sake of profit is of limited importance. The more important question is: What does the firm plan to do with its profits? It may re-invest in the production line, it may share profits with stockholders, or, among other things, the firm may decide on non-market investments.[31] This is consistent with the economic law named after J. B. Say, which states that every offer of goods for sale is an implicit demand for goods that will be received in exchange.[32] We cannot exclude goods such as political influence or "power" which a firm may receive in the exchange.

The inability to specify what constitutes primary demand for a product creates some level of uncertainty in the marketplace. In order to approximate the scope of consumer demand for its product the firm must turn to market surveys, rules of thumb, intuition based on experience, guesses (educated or not), and other available methods.[33]

Consider now an oligopolistic industry — defined as an industry comprised of a few (usually $2 \leq N < 8$) large firms and some or no small firms. Examples of such oligopolies in the United States are the automobile industry, the steel industry, the detergent industry and, of course, the cigarette industry.

The market situation of oligopoly, to be sure, is different from situations of monopoly and pure competition. Under monopoly, a single firm has only to consider the market demand schedule. In pure competition, where by definition there are numerous competing firms, each firm need not be concerned with its rivals but only with the market price. In oligopoly the situation is quite different. Each firm must take into consideration the decisions and responses of other firms in the industry.

From as early as 1838, attempts have been made to explain and predict the market behavior of firms in oligopoly and especially to determine an equilibrium solution.[34] Although 140 years have passed,

> the unsatisfactory and inconclusive state of contemporary oligopoly theory leaves an important gap in our knowledge of the operative mechanics of modern industrial economies containing a significant ingredient of private capitalism.[35]

The oligopoly problem has been studied through many economic approaches, from Cournot in 1838 to J. Friedman in 1977. The list of others who have attempted an understanding of the problem is impressive indeed: Chamberlin, Cyert and March, Markham and Fellner, to mention a few "conventionals"; Von Neumann and Morgenstern, Shubik, Nicholson, and Sherman, to mention some who utilized the tools of game theory in their investigation.[36]

Unfortunately, the collective result is either too theoretically abstract and cannot be tested empirically, or it is applicable only in a specific case. Perhaps, however, an individual approach is necessary if we wish to draw policy implications from the operation of a given oligopoly.

Firms within modern oligopolies resort to a variety of policies and strategies in their competition against each other. Apart from price strategies and output manipulations, they may compete through advertising, product changes, marketing methods and other nonprice alternatives, and/or combinations of these. Markham may have best summarized this peculiarity.

> There are many varieties of industrial structures, each exhibiting its own peculiar behavior pattern, that can be technically de-

fined as oligopoly. Some conform to Chamberlinian conjectural interdependence, others to one of several price leadership models; some give factual support to the Kink demand curve hypothesis, others exhibit reasonably flexible prices; some oligopolists appear to use sophisticated strategies, others to rely heavily on price concessions. Oligopoly is far less homogeneous than the term "few sellers" might imply.[37]

The complexity implied by this description necessitates, for the purpose of deriving some policy implications, setting some market strategies as constants or singling out a set of strategies available to the firm. Price strategy as a combative means will be set constant. This is reasonable due to the figures presented in the historical review of the cigarette industry in Chapter two and is further corroborated by Nicholls and Telser.[38] It may be, however, that this applies only to the cigarette industry and not to other oligopolies.

The constant price is a result of the nature of the product, the forms of taxation, and other fixed costs such as production and distribution. Thus, the average retail price per package was forty-five cents in the 1970s, and the average gross profit was 1.5 cents per package.[39] It seems that a firm, in order to reduce the consumer's price by one cent (i.e., a reduction of two percent) has to reduce its profit margin by sixty-six percent. Competition by price, therefore, is unpleasant and to be avoided if possible, and advertising becomes an attractive means for competition among rivals.

Advertising is a marketing strategy, which, like investment should yield present or future returns. If this were not true, firms in a given industry would not find it reasonable to employ advertising. But there exists a serious theoretical debate concerning the actual effects of advertising on consumer behavior.

Advertising may be one among many factors which influence individuals to buy a product. As a means of communication it serves two purposes: the provision of information about the availability of the product and its characteristics; and a means of persuading the consumer to buy product A and not product B.

Is advertising the single most influential factor in consumer behavior? The question is still under dispute. Galbraith, for example, argued that for the most part, consumer demand is "managed" by the producers. Advertising, he claims, especially on radio and television, becomes a prime instrument in such management.[40] This kind of "mega-manipulation" assumes that the consumer lacks the intelligence to make independent decisions. Many students of advertising disagree. Among them, Robert Solow has expressed a diametrically opposite opinion.

> I suppose . . . that it must be relatively easy to affect such decisions [decisions between alternative brands of the same product at a given price] by advertising . . . it must be hard to influence the consumer's choice between purchase of cigarettes and purchases of beer, and much harder still to influence his distribution of expenditures among such broad categories as food, clothing, automobiles, housing. It is open to legitimate doubt that advertising has any detectable affect at all on the subtotal of consumer spending or, in other words, on the choice between spending and saving.[41]

Raymond Bauer and Stephen Greyser in their study on advertising in America concluded that "advertising does not occupy a central place in people's consciousness."[42] Perhaps it captures the subconscious, or perhaps, especially for new products, advertising exploits the consumer's latent demand for a product. All this only seems to suggest that it is very easy to either overstate or understate the importance of advertising on consumers.

It is known that for certain defined population groups, no advertising can have an effect. For example, hamburger chains are not trying to reach vegetarians; certain feminine products are not advertised for men; and prosthetic devices are not, to our knowledge, advertised at all. This is partly because some products do not have advertisable features. Also, the firm is trying to sell the product, not the advertisement. The nature of the product determines, to a large degree, not only the possibility of advertising but also the amount of advertising.

Nelson, followed by Ferguson, distinguishes between "search goods" and "experience goods." Either consumers can obtain information about the quality of an item by prior inspection (shoes, for example), or they must make a purchase in order to determine the quality (a package of cigarettes, for example). The former describes search goods, the latter case experience goods. Advertisements for search goods contain direct information about the product's qualities, enabling consumers to rank alternative brands of a given product. Advertisements for experience goods simply publicize the availability of a particular brand.[43]

The frequency of advertisements for a particular product should also be considered. Repetitive advertising serves to familiarize the consumer with the name of the product. By recognizing an advertised brand, the buyer is able to reduce the time and cost of his search among the many brands available. In the case of search goods, he is able to concentrate on those goods for which he has already received information prior to the actual purchase. The information provided by advertising reduces the range of alternative brands actually investigated. In the case of experience goods, where by definition on-the-spot investigation is not possible, the same mechanisms for reducing the cost of the search operate, but with greater magnitude. Here, advertising attempts to establish a higher degree of trust between producers and customers. Trust can be established in various ways, since the customer buys the goods and services, not the advertising. This latter is aimed at reinforcing the trust in the product. For example, producers may try to provide a buyer, at every purchase, with a product of *identical* quality so that past satisfaction and experience with the product will motivate continued purchase and loyalty to the product. Some motels or fast food chains will therefore provide, regardless of their geographical location, the same style and quality of goods or services every time. This consistency helps to establish product credibility, and the individual would presumably tend to prefer the known, credible product over an unknown. Repetitive advertising reinforces this tendency.

Repetitive advertising and maintenance of quality are not only directed toward the second, third or nth encounter with the buyer. They also attempt to lure potential buyers from competitors. The logic involved here is quite simple. An individual may reason that only successful firms can afford the high cost necessary to carry repetitive messages on the various media. Success in the market usually means that many customers are buying the product, thereby generating sufficient returns for the firm, increasing its ability to allocate more resources to advertising and to the maintenance of product quality. The individual, in an attempt to minimize his risk of disappointment from the product, will tend to turn to those brands which are heavily advertised. Knowing which experience goods are heavily advertised, argue Ferguson and Nelson, is important information to the consumer because such brands are usually higher quality and better buys. In fact, experience goods are advertised three times more than search goods.[44]

A "mature market" is one where producers offer popular experience goods based on an already established consumer history or pattern of purchase. In such a market, advertising is not aimed necessarily at the expansion of the market but rather at convincing people to experiment with another brand or product at the expense of the product they usually buy. Stated from the opposite view, the purpose of advertising is to reinforce consumer loyalty to one firm's product and to create disloyalty toward other firms' products. Advertising in a mature market is therefore a strategy designed to increase and/or defend the market share of a particular brand.[45]

Thus, in a mature oligopolistic market, sales depend not only on the amount a firm invests in advertising, nor only on the effectiveness of the campaign, but also on the amount and effectiveness of the advertising of other firms.[46]

Assume that such a market is stable in the sense that total market sales expand more or less by the same ratio as the population. Assume also that all profit-maximizing firms have the same base of information with regard to the level of demand for a product. Finally assume that all firms are able to deliver advertised messages with the same degree of success. A rational decision maker will invest in advertising as long as he can expect returns. In a two-firm market, the sales of a given firm are a function of the advertising outlay of one as compared to that of its competitor. An increase in one's market share can be represented in the functional form as follows:

$$\Delta S_A = f\left(A^A / (A^{B*}), A^B\right)$$

and for the second firm:

$$\Delta S_B = f(A^B/(A^{A^*}), A^A)$$

where:

ΔS_A and ΔS_B denote increases in the market share of the sales of firm A and B respectively;

A^A and A^B denote the actual spending in advertising of firms A and B respectively;

(A^A/A^{B^*}) denotes the actual spending on advertising of firm A given its expectation of how much firm B will spend.

Firm A may have a greater or equal share of the market at any point prior to the decision to advertise $(S_A \geq S_B)$. If firm A tries to increase its share, it may do so only at the expense of B's share $(S_A + \Delta S_A > S_B - \Delta S_B)$ and likewise for B $(S_A - \Delta S_A < S_B + \Delta S_B)$. This situation is termed "zero-sum" in game theory. It is clear that each aggressive move taken by one firm will result in a response by another firm. Thus, in a stable market, where the firms' decision makers are rational and are calculating their strategies from a similar information base, we should expect that the optimal level of investment in advertising will be the point where $A^A = A^B$. Thus, in order to maintain at least their relative size in the market, i.e., $S_A \geq S_B$, it follows that the firms need not advertise at all.[47] However, the fact remains that firms do advertise.

Two plausible explanations for such "irrational" behavior are the uncertainty of consumer behavior and the possibility of having miscalculated the opponents' expected behavior. The lowest equilibrium point of expenditure (zero) is therefore not met in reality. However, do firms arrive at the upper equilibrium point where the cost of advertising meets its returns?

Firms recognize that if each would hold back its level of expenditure, then each would increase its rate of profit without endangering its market position. Since it is illegal to collude at the market level, they must find indirect means to inform their competitors of future plans so that calculations of "expected" investment on all sides will be more accurate. The more accurate the calculation, the more likely it is that one firm will not trigger a chain reaction in advertising expenditures. Thus, all firms will be able to maintain a lower advertising level, secure their market situation, and enjoy higher profits. This could generally be accomplished through public announcements and releases of data concerning sales and expenditures in trade journals or other public forms.

In the cigarette industry, the trade journals and publications that allow this flow of information are *Tobacco Reporter, Advertising Age, Printers' Ink, Marketing/Communication,* and *National Advertising Investment* (LNA). Releases of information to *Fortune,* the *Wall Street Journal, Business Week,* and the *New York Times,* for example, reach even wider audiences.

This type of friendly competition is more beneficial than aggressive methods. Shubik, observing the competition in the cigarette industry during the 1950s, wrote: "they [the six largest firms] all have sufficient resources . . . hence there is no payoff to be gained by indulging in fight-to-the-death struggles."[48]

When profit levels are high, the market situation looks attractive to outsiders who may try to corner some of the profit themselves. This establishes a threat to which existing companies may respond in various ways. They can lower the price of the product and/or increase advertising expenditures. Alternatively, depending on financial and legal conditions, they may attempt to absorb the new competitors.[49] By far the best alternative is to maneuver passage of a regulation which essentially bars or removes incentives for new entries. The high level of profit would still be maintained. Indeed, Stigler argues that one of the two most important objectives of industry is to achieve control over the entry of new rivals (the other being direct subsidy of money).[50]

The first part of this chapter concluded that public regulation must be based on or deduced from some normative notion of the "public interest." The following section shows that the regulatory outcome may benefit the industry.

Market Situation B

Suppose now that it was determined that the consumption of a given product causes negative externalities. The existence of such externali-

ties may constitute the normative ground for government intervention. Although this is a necessary condition for intervention, it
is often not sufficient. In fact, some industries whose products
cause such externalities are regulated while others are not. This
may depend on the harm perceived to result from the product, but
of equal or greater consequence is the articulation of demand by the
concerned government to intervene on behalf of the public. The
government is then often "forced" into the conflictual situation.

Articulation of demand implies that a concerned group is able to
make it known that it is not satisfied with the current state of
affairs with regard to a particular product. The message is publicly
promulgated by the media. The government may or may not be
partner to such publicity. When it is, it usually adds authenticity
to the message. The reader may recall from Chapter two that during
the 1960s, and especially in the years 1964 and 1968 to 1970, large
amounts of "negative information" regarding the influence of
smoking on health were transmitted to the public through the
media. Such additional information creates a more difficult decision
for the consumer than he was faced with in Market Situation A.
He may ignore or incorporate this additional component in his
utility function. Suppose that in Market Situation A a given individual's utility function is composed of three elements, x, y, and z,
each with its own weight. The new information (w), in situation B,
enters his or her utility function negatively; thus,

$$U_i = ((x, y, z) - (w))$$

On the aggregate, actual consumer behavior may change. Individuals may reduce their level of consumption, alter their taste, or
drop out of the market. "The edge of the market" — in the cigarette
case, "marginal smokers" — should be affected more than others.

Firms may logically respond by challenging the credibility of the
source; by informing the public that the "alleged" existence of
externalities was not satisfactorily proven; by offering new products
which presumably minimize the externalities; by convincing other
recognized sources not to participate with the "enemy"; and by
moving into other businesses.[51] Such endeavors are expensive, and
success is not guaranteed.

In addition, the response may take the form of a seemingly contradictory situation, as manifested by the case of the cigarette industry during the 1960s: the external threat brought about the formation of a "grand coalition" of all the firms on the political level, but simultaneously, an advertising war broke out. However, these seemingly contradictory acts actually complemented each other.

The chain of events began with the uncertainty that occurs at the economic level. This, it was argued, was due mainly to the negative information being transferred to the public. The greater the quantity of negative information, the more it may affect consumer behavior. Since firms may be affected unequally, their market position becomes insecure. They must respond to possible alterations in taste preferences by introducing new brands and increasing advertising expenditures. In addition, the calculation of rivals' behavior, relatively close before, is less accurate now. Consumer behavior is less predictable. This creates an unsatisfactory situation for the firms.

In more formal terms it can be said that the firms have reached a non-Pareto optimal point. A Pareto optimal situation may be defined in different ways. In our context it means the following: one situation, one social state, or one alternative is better than another if every individual (firm) feels it is better according to his own values. Since a non-Pareto optimal outcome is inherent in the "prisoners' dilemma," we can use this game to elucidate some properties of this situation.

Assume the following: (a) Advertising is an effective strategy for competing for market share. (b) There are diminishing marginal returns to advertising. Suppose that in a two-firm market each firm has two alternative ways of utilizing its advertising strategy. The first firm can maintain a low-cost strategy (L1) or a high-cost strategy (H1). Likewise, the second firm can utilize (L2) and (H2) respectively. The interest of the firm will be served when it maintains the low-cost strategy only if its competitor follows suit. Thus they would both maintain their share of the market. However, if one firm maintains a high-cost strategy while its rival follows a low-cost strategy, the former increases its share of the market at the expense

TABLE C. The "Prisoners' Dilemma" of Advertising in Oligopoly

		Firm 2	
		Low Cost (L2)	High Cost (H2)
Firm 1	Low Cost (L1)	20, 20	10, 30-C
	High Cost (H1)	30-C, 10	20-C, 20-C

The entries in each cell are hypothetical numbers which denote the percentage of market share each firm acquires maintaining one or another strategy. We use the concept of market share in the text as a *surrogate* for profit, (see reference 43 to this chapter). Since profit level will be reduced with the increased cost of advertising (C), this cost is deducted from the above numbers, thus generating a situation which resembles the prisoners' dilemma.

of the latter. Of course, both firms are aware of these possibilities and since they cannot legally convey their strategies to each other, or since their signals may be distorted because of the high level of uncertainty, they are both locked in a situation which resembles the prisoner's dilemma, as shown in Table C.[52]

Thus, if Firm 1 maintains the low-cost strategy, Firm 2 should maintain H2, the high-cost strategy, increasing its market share by ten percent. Similarly, if Firm 1 maintains H1, Firm 2 should again retain H2, thus securing its percentage share of the market. Regardless of the strategy chosen by Firm 1, Firm 2 maximizes its utility by choosing a high-cost strategy. Once this is established, Firm 1 must also retain its expensive strategy. Consequently, a competitive equilibrium H1, H2 results, which is expensive for both, although they both retain the same market share held under the "non-competitive" equilibrium.

Since presumably this conclusion has not escaped the firms, there should be a way to return to the more attractive equilibrium L1, L2. If the game is played over a period of time, the firms themselves may arrive at a solution. Meanwhile, however, some firms may find themselves in serious financial straits. Therefore, a solution at the political level becomes more desirable for the firms concerned. In more formal terms, we may say that the political solution was preferred by all firms involved in the conflict and was the solution which could bring them closer to their Pareto optimal point.

There is less uncertainty in the political arena. The firm knows, for example, the ground rules established by the constitution. Some industries, especially the important economic industries, may have past experience and established relations with several governmental units.[53] They can assess the strength of the opposition and where it is located. The firms can thus maneuver the struggle from one political stage to another, in an attempt to acquire the best possible alternative solution or regulation.[54]

In the cigarette case, the government's "salient" solution, in Schelling's terms,[55] was presumably imported from abroad through a process known as "diffusion of innovation."[56] That is, since it was adopted in other countries as a solution to the smoking-and-health controversy it was accepted also in the United States. Thus, in 1971 the United States, like Great Britain (1965) and Italy (1962), banned the advertising of cigarettes on television and radio. The prohibition, an outside force, forced all firms to move from the high-cost equilibrium to the low-cost one. The regulation was even more attractive to the industry if we consider the fact that by taking cigarette advertising off the air, the antismoking forces lost an important channel for influencing the public. Hence, less negative information was transmitted by the media to the public as compared with the years of the operation of the Fairness Doctrine.

Furthermore, this solution reduced the saliency of the smoking-and-health controversy but still left the printed media open as a channel for promoting "safer" low tar and nicotine cigarettes. And, returning to an earlier point, the industry also gained an effective barrier against potential new entries into the market. Three students of industrial advertising reinforce this notion: ". . . it is not surprising, therefore, that advertising decreases monopoly over price. Advertising probably also reduces barriers to entry."[57] "Advertising is a means of entry. Prohibition of advertising is a barrier."[58] "Advertising is frequently a means of entry and a sign of competition. This agrees with the view that advertising is an important source of information."[59]

If this is true, then the logical question which follows is, why is there no record of new firms entering the market when the product was fully advertised? The reason is presumably grounded in the fact that announcements of a correlation between smoking and health, and the bitter competition among the firms which reduced profit margins, discouraged potential investors. This "could hardly attract even a mildly prudent businessman."[60] The reader may recall from Chapter two that successful entries (i.e., Philip Morris and Brown and Williamson) had been made prior to this controversy.

Since advertising is essential to the maintenance of effective competition, an interesting paradox was created by the ban. The Sherman Act and other antitrust regulations prohibit the cooperation of firms on the market level. The firms had to move to the political level where such restraints do not exist. Operating on that level enabled the industry to acquire a regulation which essentially restricts the free competition which is required at the economic level. Hence, by viewing public regulation as a process, it was possible to demonstrate how one regulation may breed another regulation which counteracts the first.

The ready conclusion is that although it is counterintuitive, *the ban imposed on the advertising of cigarettes was in the industry's interest.*

SUMMARY

This theoretical discussion started by considering public regulation as a process which is essentially political, where each regulation is an episode in a conflict between political coalitions and where the outcome favors the industry. Then the nature of competition in an oligopolistic market was explicated with the cigarette industry in mind. It was also argued that the regulation of advertising is consistent with the objectives of the industry as a profit maximizer. The chapter was concluded by revealing an apparent paradox, wherein under certain dynamic conditions one regulation may generate a second counterproductive one. The burden of proof falls, of course, on us. The next chapter will bring evidence from the cigarette case to support the following:

1. Advertising in the cigarette industry is not a means of market expansion but rather a competitive strategy employed by the firm to increase market share.
2. Antiadvertising is an effective means of reducing the size of the market.
3. The cigarette firms, as profit maximizers, were better off after the 1971 regulation than prior to it.

In Chapter five it is shown, among other things, that the industry was aware, long before regulation, that this move would be beneficial to its purposes.

THE·SERPENT·CIGARETTE·

FOUR

The Effects of Regulation:
An Empirical Assessment

FOUR

The previous chapter dealt with the dynamics of regulation in general terms. It was argued that in the case of the cigarette industry public intervention in the market activities of the firms involved was not necessarily incompatible with the interests of those same firms. Two examples of such intervention were the requirement of a warning label on each package of cigarettes and the prohibition on the advertising of the product on the broadcast media.

The objective of this chapter is to provide empirical support for this conclusion. More specifically, the statements set out at the end of Chapter three will be addressed and included in a formal model. Recall that these statements or hypotheses dealt with the purpose of advertising, the effects of antiproduct advertising (or what we called negative information), and the nature and the outcomes of the regulatory process. The rationale for the construction of the following model, the considerations dealt with, and inferences drawn from the test conducted will follow as well.

MODEL CONSTRUCTION

It is often difficult for the policy analyst to determine the true intent of the policy maker. In many cases, and for a variety of reasons, the goals to be achieved by a given policy act are not explicit. The objective of the policy makers — the regulators — in the cigarette case was not explicitly stated during much of the controversy of the 1960s. Senator Neuberger, long-time opponent of the cigarette industry, noted this phenomenon during the 1965 debate over the labelling bill. She said, "The impact on the public . . . would be greater if what Congress really wants to do . . . decrease cigarette consumption — was specifically spelled out."[1]

To be sure, the concern of public officials presumably focused on the negative effects on health generated by cigarette smoking. Thus, regulations should be assessed with reference to the changes occurring at the social health level.

There are several possible ways to construct indicators of health. Here it is explicitly posited that the regulations were intended to decrease the level of cigarette consumption. By so defining the policy makers' goal and by using level of consumption as a health indicator, a negative linear relationship between the number of cigarettes smoked and health is assumed. Confidence in this assumption is corroborated by the findings of the Surgeon General's Advisory Committee on Smoking and Health, which were made public on January 11, 1964. Specifically, the report concluded that in the many retrospective studies conducted, smoking-related symptoms, signs and illness "increase with the amount of smoking and decrease after cessation of smoking."[2] Prospective studies also demonstrated that "in general, the greater the number of cigarettes smoked daily, the higher the death rate."[3] This relationship was reinforced by many other studies conducted after 1964.[4] Perhaps the most straightforward expression of this negative relationship between smoking and health was made by Canadian policy makers, who required the labelling of each cigarette package with the following warning: "Health and Welfare Canada advises that danger to health increases with the amount smoked — avoid inhaling."[5]

The level of cigarette consumption is determined, of course, not only by the effect of the regulation but by other factors as well. The policy maker may be able to directly affect or manipulate some of these factors, while others may not be under his control. These latter nevertheless must be included in any fully specified model of the level of consumption. It is thus proper to identify those factors which are manipulable by policy makers and those which are not. Formally it can be said that the level of cigarette consumption (the dependent variable) is explained by, or is a function of, policy manipulable and non-manipulable factors (the independent variables).

In the theoretical discussion in Chapter three, some of the independent variables which were said to affect consumption have already been identified, i.e., regulation and the marketing practices of the industry, especially product advertising. Also as outlined, the price of the product and personal disposable income are to be considered explanatory variables. Yet another explanatory variable must be included as well. Although it may appear in many forms, it is labelled here "habit formation."

An explanation of the meaning of each variable, the rationale for inclusion and the form of specification of the model variables will follow the formal presentation of the model in the next section.

MODEL SPECIFICATION

Formally, the model that provides the test for the theoretical discussion may be presented in linear additive form as follows:

$$Y_t = a + \beta_1 Y_{t-1} + \beta_2 X_{1t} + \beta_3 X_{2t} + \beta_4 D_1 + \beta_5 D_2 + U_t \quad (1.1)$$

where:

Y_t = sales of cigarettes in units per capita at time t

Y_{t-1} = lagged variable of Y_t (i.e., sales of cigarettes in units per capita in prior year)

X_{1t} = advertising expenditures on cigarettes at time t in deflated dollars (base year 1952)

X_{2t} = effective price of cigarettes (i.e., the fraction of an average person's disposable income spent on the product) at time t

D_1 = dummy variable — the Fairness Doctrine — has a value of (1) between 1968 and 1970 and (0) otherwise

D_2 = dummy variable — Antismoking Activities (ANSA), excluding the Fairness Doctrine — has a value of (1) from 1964 on, and (0) prior to it

Variables D_1, D_2, and X_2 are policy manipulable while Y_{t-1} and X_1 are not, as the following discussion explicates.

The Policy Manipulable Variables

The policy maker may be able to affect consumption by using the tool of regulation. In the case of the cigarette industry, the regulators chose primarily to alter the kind of information provided by the industry about the product. They required that the industry provide additional information about the product (i.e., warning label requirements). They prohibited the advertising of the products in the broadcast media. Further, by means of the Fairness Doctrine, the government subsidized a direct attack against smoking in the media. While these were the principal strategies employed, policy makers could also attempt to affect consumption by manipulating the price of the product through taxation. The impact of each of these strategies will be examined.

Antismoking activities (ANSA) and the Fairness Doctrine. The regulations imposed by the government on the industry amounted to the creation of negative information about the product. It was previously argued that this information affects the satisfaction a smoker receives from the act of smoking. Consequently, the consumer may alter his taste for the product, reduce the number of cigarettes he consumes, or even stop consuming altogether. Between 1968 and 1970, when the Fairness Doctrine was implemented, there was a direct and deliberate attempt to affect consumer preference and reduce cigarette consumption through negative information.

Negative information was also generated indirectly through the activities of various public bodies involved in the conflict. For example, the public was presumably influenced by the 1964 Surgeon General's report and the labelling acts of 1965 and 1969. These indirect messages clearly contributed to the atmosphere against smoking and cannot be ignored. Consequently, two separate variables which incorporate the information concerning both the direct and the indirect messages against smoking were designed.

The construction of the variable representing direct attempts to influence consumer preference was relatively simple. The Fairness Doctrine was implemented in 1968 and removed by 1971, resulting in three years of deliberate policy intervention. However, difficulties in obtaining figures on the expenditure of the antismoking coalition during those years necessitated the use of a dummy (binary) variable for the Fairness Doctrine. Thus the value of (1) will represent the years of intervention and (0) otherwise.

To construct the variable representing indirect negative information the concept of "regulatory acts as a process" was utilized. The variable includes all public intervention with regard to smoking, apart from the regulation of the Fairness Doctrine, in a single binary variable. This variable is called "antismoking activities" (ANSA); the value of (1) is assigned to it from 1964, and (0) previous to 1964, when the smoking issue was not on the government agenda.

The expectation is that the ANSA will have an inverse effect on consumption. This expectation can be represented graphically as shown in Figure two.

If one adds to this the expectation that the Fairness Doctrine will also have a detrimental effect on consumption, the combined expected effects on consumption can be represented in graphical form as shown in Figure three.

Note, however, that the graphical figures are merely an expression of the expected negative effects on consumption indicated by the operation of the dummy variables in the time series. Since

FIGURE 2
The Expected Effect of ANSA on the Level of Consumption
After 1964 (controlling for all other factors)

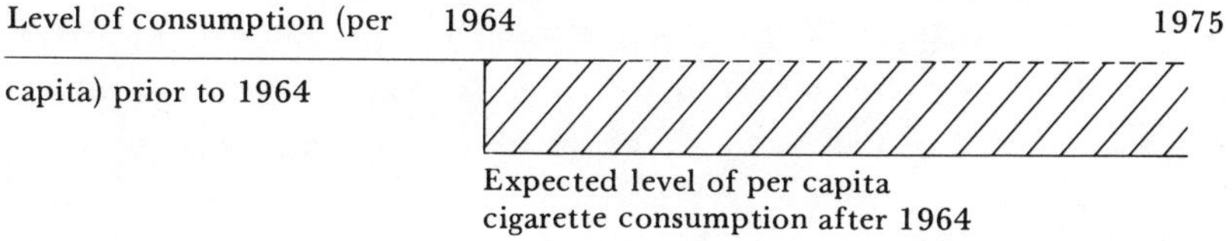

Level of consumption (per   1964   1975

capita) prior to 1964

Expected level of per capita
cigarette consumption after 1964

FIGURE 3
The Expected Effect of ANSA and the Fairness Doctrine
on the Level of Consumption After 1964 (controlling all other factors)

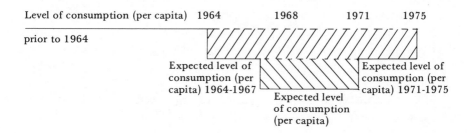

Level of consumption (per capita)   1964   1968   1971   1975

prior to 1964

Expected level of
consumption (per
capita) 1964-1967

Expected level
of consumption
(per capita)

Expected level of
consumption (per
capita) 1971-1975

the variable assumes the value of (1) in the years of intervention, and, as previously stated, it is expected that they will have an adverse effect on consumption, the graphs show only a reduction in one "step" in the level of consumption. This seemingly unified level of reduction is presented for purposes of convenience and clarity of presentation. The real effects of the regulations will, however, be estimated by utilizing the techniques of "impact multipliers" as shown in the analytical section to follow.

The impact multiplier technique is a useful tool for the assessment of the effects of intervention and their magnitude during the years of implementation. Moreover, since the negative information generated by public intervention did not disappear immediately after implementation of the acts, and since some effects, presumably decreasing, were carried over even after the period of their execution, the technique helps determine the magnitude of their effects over a longer period of time. It will also indicate the time when one can expect them not to have any further substantial influence on consumption.

Effective price of cigarettes. As outlined in Chapter three, combinations of factors determine the actual purchase of a product. The price of a product and personal disposable income are important factors that should be taken into consideration if one wishes to understand what contributes to the level of product consumption.

The price of a product is clearly a variable that can be manipulated by the policy maker. He can increase or decrease the price by simply taxing the product or removing existing taxes. Disposable income, on the other hand, particularly in the case of cigarettes, is not likely to be manipulated. The reason for this is that the smoking-and-health issue has only a secondary position on the national agenda. In times of war or other national crises, the policy maker may, no doubt, consider the possibility of affecting personal income by imposing restrictive measures on individual income. However, in the smoking-and-health policy area, even if it was determined that as personal income increases so does cigarette consumption, one can be sure that the ensuing policy strategy would not be to reduce income.

On the other hand, the consumer apparently does consider disposable income and product price when making his decision with regard to the purchasing of a product. He may ask himself, "Given my free income, how much money can I spend this month (week, year) on product X?" The smaller his disposable income and the higher the price of the commodity, the less he will tend to buy. Alteration in the level of his free income and in the price of the product will determine the "effective price of the product."[6]

The interest here is not in the separate effect of price and income or consumption (which are usually found to affect consumption in opposite ways) but rather in the combined effect — i.e., the fraction of disposable income an average person spends on the product in question.[7] From a policy point of view, constructing a variable which takes these two components into account has a great intuitive and descriptive appeal. It will enable one to ascertain, given the level of personal disposable income (the non-manipulable element of the variable), how much the policy maker might increase the price of a product (by means of a tax or otherwise) in order to successfully affect consumption.

The information on personal disposable income is taken from government sources,[8] while data concerning the price of cigarettes is extracted from information published by the industry.[9] However, since price variations exist among the various states due to differences in taxation policies, the explanation of how to determine the price of cigarettes for the United States deserves a more detailed elaboration. This will be found at the end of the following section.

The Non-Manipulable Variables

This section addresses itself to the explanation of variables over which the policy maker has limited or no control.

Habit formation. There is general agreement that smoking is primarily a psychological habituation, although one cannot rule out the possibility that it is also a physiological addiction.[10] If habit is an important part of consumer behavior, it would clearly be unwise to ignore its effect. In terms of the theoretical discussion advanced in Chapter three, this factor is close in spirit to "product loyalty."

In the aggregate it can be said that loyalty to the product (as distinguished from loyalty to a particular brand) can be manifested by the fact that a certain percentage of last year's smokers will return to the market this year. Also on the aggregate level, it may be reasoned that consumers, by revealing their choice to remain or to leave the smoking population, are bringing with them the necessary information regarding general economic conditions in the market. Those who are more susceptible to economic fluctuations, and/or were affected by the negative information generated by the regulations (i.e., usually the marginal smokers) may exit, while others will stay. Thus, while the regulator is attempting to manipulate the means under his control, he cannot manipulate the past, i.e., the history of consumption.

The history of consumption can be accounted for by simply lagging the dependent variable (i.e., level of cigarette consumption expressed in terms of units of cigarettes sold in a given year t). Thus, the lagged dependent variable was designed to be a "once and for all" lag.[11] This means that although what happened three or four years ago may have some effect on our decision today, it is only reasonable to assume that the greatest weight should be given to what "happened" in the most recent time interval (in this case, last year). The diminishing values of subsequent effects are thus represented only once by the lagged variable. Hence, not many lagged variables are carried over from one year to another and enough degrees of freedom are left for the estimation process.[12]

The number of product units sold is an important statistic for executives. If more units are sold this year as compared to last year, then all other things being equal, the profit-seeking firm will be better off. But profit considerations are not necessarily important to the public policy maker. He is presumably interested in knowing how his decision affected the smoking population. It is not the total consumption that he considers but the per capita level of consumption. If the population increased at a faster rate than consumption, then, without controlling for this rise, the policy maker might believe that his policies are affecting behavior.[13]

A decision has to be made, however, as to which age group should be included in the "percapitization" procedure. Various studies on cigarette consumption have selected different minimum ages, ranging from fourteen to twenty, while other studies have included the total population.[14] A recent study conducted for the American Cancer Society reveals that "the problem is that most teenagers — boys and girls — now start to smoke before they are in junior high."[15] Had we chosen an adult population (eighteen years of age and older), we could have been ignoring the fact that in years more and more young people have been entering the smoking population. On the other hand, had we chosen fourteen to be the relevant age, we would have encountered the problem of determining whose disposable income was involved in the purchase of the product, the children's or that of their parents.

The decision was to perform the test on models utilizing both sets of information — once for the population eighteen years old and older, and once for the population fourteen years old and older. As it turns out, the results did not differ greatly from one age group to the other.

The data for various age groups was compiled from *Population Estimates and Projections.*[16] Information with regard to the industry sales figures includes only the leading cigarette brands, as ranked in the various issues of *Advertising Age,* during the period from 1954 to 1975.[17] The year 1954 was selected as the lower boundary of the observations partly because at around that time the industry tested and launched its filter brands. The major filter brands of the 1960s and 1970s were introduced between 1954 and 1956.[18]

Thirty-seven brands were thus ranked during the period observed. The number of leading brands for each firm during that time period is distributed as follows: American, eight; Philip Morris, seven; R. J. Reynolds, seven; Liggett and Myers, Brown and Williamson, and P. Lorillard, five each. Aggregate information about non-leading brands is provided in Appendix C. For comparison, out of fifty-four non-leading brands for which information was gathered on sales and/or advertising expenditures, American had fifteen; Brown and Williamson had fourteen; Philip Morris had nine; R. J. Reynolds, Liggett and Myers, and P. Lorillard carried five each.

The reason for excluding the non-leading brands corresponds to the notion of market "maturity." It is often difficult to determine whether a non leading brand was introduced nationally and still failed to capture a reasonable market share or whether it was only tested in selected markets. The information compiled from *Advertising Age* covered nationwide brands. The combined totals of the leading brands' share of the market was no lower than ninety-seven percent.

In some instances, especially in the 1950s, certain leading brands were excluded from the *Advertising Age* rankings. Since the products were sold and advertised, it was decided to continue the observation of these brands in the following years. Sales figures were taken from Harry M. Wooten's "Special Report" in *Printers' Ink* and from the "Special Maxwell Reports."[19]

Figure four shows the time series for total cigarette sales (leading brands) between the years 1954 and 1975. It also shows a comparison of sales per capita of cigarettes during that period using the two different age groups, eighteen years old and over, and fourteen years old and over.

FIGURE 4
Cigarette Sales Per Capita
(Ages 14 and Over, 18 and Over) Leading Brands, 1954-1975

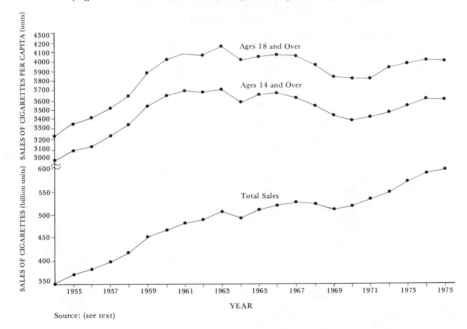

Source: (see text)

Industry advertising of cigarettes. The policy maker can affect the kind of information the industry transmits to the public through advertising. Indeed, some restrictions on the content of cigarette advertising were imposed, especially during the 1960s. But the policy maker cannot, short of banning advertising from one or all media, block the channels of information used by the industry to inform consumers about the availability of the product, and to enable the public to recognize brands. In this respect, and as long as some means of communication are legally open to the industry, advertising may be partly considered a non-manipulable variable, as far as the policy maker is concerned.

The advertising variable in model (1.1) represents aggregate industry expenditures on cigarette advertising in the various media. It has been argued that the effect of advertising should be measured in terms of messages rather than dollar expenditures.[20] Such data, however, is very difficult to obtain in the United States. Moreover, it is argued later that even if one could arrive at a figure for "minutes of advertisement per number of listeners" or "lines of text per reader," the intellectual gain may be only marginal.[21]

Approximations of how many people have been exposed to a broadcast message or how many readers (beyond circulation figures) are exposed to the advertisements in a newspaper are naturally extremely unreliable. A simple example will illustrate the difficulties. A portion of cigarette advertising is accomplished through the medium of billboards; but even if one could find the density of pedestrian and vehicular traffic in a given area, one would have to make some assumptions concerning the proportion of people who look above their heads when they pass near a particular sign.

On the other hand, if one follows the logic of the market, one may be quite close to the approximation of the real value of advertisements. It is known, for instance, that advertising time on prime time television is more expensive than "fringe" period advertising. Likewise, renting a billboard in Times Square is, presumably, more costly than using a similar board on Route 96 from Rochester to Binghamton. Although it is often forgotten, price is a good indicator of value. The cost of advertising is a reflection of the value of the advertisements in terms of the actual or potential exposure under time and space constraints.

Advertising Age provides information about total expenditures on advertising for the leading brands. As with the information regarding sales figures, not all leading brands which appeared in the 1950s had a continuous ranking in the 1960s or 1970s. The information concerning such brands was thus complemented by figures taken from *Leading National Advertisers (LNA).*[22] The data acquired from *LNA* also provided a detailed account of the industry's expenditures in each medium, that is, broadcast and print.

The reason for structuring these separate variables was to facilitate judgment whether the uncertainty caused by putting the smoking issue on the government agenda was reflected in the level of industry expenditures; i.e., the fluctuation and increase in the amount spent between periods and across media.

The broadcasting variable is a combination of industry expenditures on network television, network radio, spot television, and spot radio. Similarly, expenditures in the print medium reflect the combined cost of advertising in magazines, newspaper supplements, and outdoor ads.[23] Categories such as "general promotion," "multi-product ads," and "premium offers" were also incorporated as long as a brand name was associated with them.

Figure five shows the combined and separate expenditures on advertising of cigarettes in each medium. The reader can observe the high increase in industry expenditures on the broadcasting media between the years 1962 and 1970. It is also evident from the graph that during this period there were large yearly fluctuations in the broadcasting media while expenditures on print were much more stable. The fluctuations in the major advertising media correspond to the situation of uncertainty described in Chapter three. It is also clear that after the 1971 ban on broadcasting the industry shifted most of its advertising budget to print. Nonetheless, expenditures in 1975 did not reach the level of 1963. This fact, combined with increases in the sales of cigarettes after 1971, already begins to suggest that the industry may have been better off after the ban as compared to the period from 1954 to 1970.

The discussion in Chapter three concerning the purpose of advertising is not expressed in terms of one or another medium. Hence model (1.1) was constructed and the tests were performed with regard to the advertising of cigarettes in general. It seems

FIGURE 5
Expenditures On Print Ads, Broadcasting Ads, and
Total Advertising Expenditures, 1954-1975

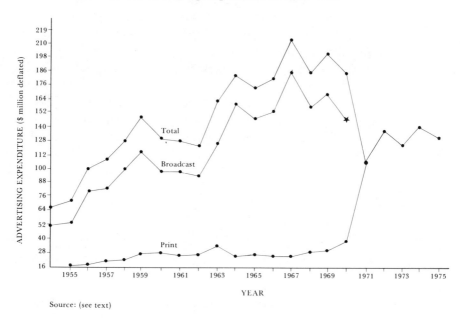

Source: (see text)

reasonable to assume that the objective of advertising (i.e., competition over market share) did not change after 1971. The same objective is being pursued by the firms through different means. The test therefore will reflect this information regarding total expenditures on advertising.

Since the power of the dollar in the 1960s or the 1970s is not the same as its power in the 1950s, all figures expressed in terms of money had to be converted to a uniform base and had to be deflated. For convenience 1952 was chosen as a base year. Thus, all dollar figures are expressed in terms of that year. For the discounting process the Consumer Price Index was used as a deflator.[24] The advertising figures, as well as price and disposable figures, were deflated accordingly.

We turn now to a discussion of how to arrive at a uniform price of cigarettes for the United States and some of the problems encountered in the determination of this price.

Determining the price of cigarettes. The price of cigarettes is a combination of three factors — the price of the product itself, federal tax, and state tax.[25] The average retail price of the cigarette package, as well as annual per capita sales in each state, is given in the publication *The Tax Burden on Tobacco.*[26] In order to arrive at a unified price for the United States, those figures have to be weighted by the population of each state (including the District of Columbia).[27] First, the quantity of cigarettes sold in each state, *q,* was determined by multiplying the per capita figures of sales by the population in each state. Once *q* was determined, the following procedure was utilized in order to arrive at an average retail price for the United States:

$$P_{at} = \frac{\Sigma_1^{51} q_{it} P_{it}}{\Sigma_1^{51} q_t}$$

where:

P_{at} =   weighted average retail price of a cigarette package at time *t*

q_{it} =   number of cigarette packages sold in state *i* at time *t*

P_{it} =   average retail price of a cigarette package in state *i* at time *t*

q_t =   number of cigarette packages sold at time *t*

Appendix D shows the prices of a package of cigarettes from 1954 to 1975. Although the preceding formula represents the price of a product in a given year, it contains one shortcoming (which appears, of course, in all other attempts to estimate the price of cigarettes). The problem is that the non-uniformity of state taxes influences the pattern of cigarette consumption. If one moves from the national level, where the demand for cigarettes is generally assumed to be relatively inelastic, to the state level, one can observe that where prices are generally higher, due to taxation, consumption per capita is lower. Can it be said that the local demand for cigarettes is highly elastic while the "universal" demand is relatively inelastic?

In order to examine this question the following procedure was utilized: neighboring states such as New Hampshire and Massachusetts, Oregon and Washington, South and North Carolina, Indiana and Illinois were paired. Then the so-called Interocular Trauma Test was employed. The literal meaning of this test is that the researcher becomes aware of the meaning of his data when the conclusion hits him between the eyes.[28] The results should become evident on presentation of the pairs as shown in Tables D and E.

TABLE D. A Comparison between the Number of Cigarette Packages Sold per Capita and State Taxes in Massachusetts and New Hampshire, 1970-1975

	Massachusetts		New Hampshire	
Year	Per Capita Sales (Packages)	State Tax (Cents)	Per Capita Sales (Packages)	State Tax (Cents)
1970	124.3	12	265.7	7
1971	121.4	16	278.0	8.5
1972	117.9	16	296.2	11
1973	121.2	16	279.0	11
1974	124.3	16	169.8	11
1975	126.1	16	269.1	11

Source: Tobacco Tax Council, *Tax Burden on Tobacco,* vol. 2 (Richmond, Virginia, 1976).

TABLE E. A Comparison between the Number of Cigarette Packages Sold per Capita and State Taxes in Oregon and Washington, 1970-1975

	Washington		Oregon	
Year	Per Capita Sales (Packages)	State Tax (Cents)	Per Capita Sales (Packages)	State Tax (Cents)
1970	96.7	11	157.0	4
1971	97.0	16	157.0	4
1972	88.5	16	160.4	9
1973	91.0	16	155.3	9
1974	98.6	16	155.8	9
1975	99.5	16	154.4	9

Source: Tobacco Tax Council, *Tax Burden on Tobacco,* vol. 2 (Richmond, Virginia, 1976).

It appears clear from these tables and from other pairs not shown here that low state taxation is associated with high consumption. The magnitude of the differences between the pairs is also very striking. It seems improbable that an average New Hampshire resident (low state tax) smokes more than twice as much as his friend from Massachusetts. Since this pattern appears for each low-high tax pair, one must conclude that citizens from Massachusetts or other high tax states were shopping in New Hampshire or other low tax states.[29] Alternatively, cigarettes were being "buttlegged," or smuggled from low-tax to high-tax states, an act which is against the law. If a citizen shops in one state and consumes at home in another, he is violating the law. The ready conclusion must be that differentiations in state tax policies (i.e., price regulation) cause massive contempt for the law.

When constructing the effective price variable, these shortcomings were considered. The variable was converted into an index by multiplying it by one hundred. Thus, the results of the test, which will be presented in the next section, appear for this variable as a one percent change in the level of the index.

THE TESTED MODEL

Empirical support for the theoretical discussion advanced in Chapter three can be derived from testing model (1.1). Since the determination of the relevant age group was left open, the model was tested twice, once for each age group. Model (2.1) presents the results of the test when the population of those eighteen and older was considered, while model (2.2) incorporates the population aged fourteen and older.

The reader may note that both models utilize the instrumental variable technique, suggested by Hibbs as a way to minimize the possible effects of autocorrelation among the disturbance terms in the estimation process; that is, since the models include the lagged variable $Y_t - 1$, and the possibility of autocorrelation exists, this situation may lead, among other things, to the "suppression" of the significance of other independent variables.[30] The instrumental variable assists the researcher in detecting and "correcting" significant autoregressive processes.[31] Such processes were not detected, however, in the tests, suggesting that the model is well specified. First, a code for the tables containing the information about the tests is provided. Presentation and analysis will follow.

A code for the tables:

SPC18 = sales of cigarettes in units per capita, population of those eighteen and older at time t

SPC14 = same as SPC18 for population of those fourteen and older

LSPC18 = SPC18 in the prior year, time $t - 1$

LSPC14 = SPC14 in the prior year, time $t - 1$

EPINX18 = Effective Price Index, ratio of per capita disposable income and weighted average price of a cigarette package, population of those eighteen and older, deflated by CPI, base year 1952 (figures in units of cigarettes per one percent change in the index)

EPINX14 = same as EPINX18 for population of those fourteen and older

FD = Fairness Doctrine, dummy, has a value of (1) between 1968 and 1970 and (0) otherwise

ANSA = antismoking activities, has a value of (0) until 1964 and (1) after

ADDEF = advertising expenditures of the cigarette industry, in all media, in deflated dollars, base year 1952

S = level of significance, SE = standard error, T = T statistics

DF = degrees of freedom, D = Durbin-Watson test for autocorrelation.

Table F shows the estimates of the parameters of the principal model (1.1) for the two age groups, i.e., model (2.1) for the older population and model (2.2) for the younger.

TABLE F.   Estimates of the Parameters of the Principal Models

Model 2.1   (Corrected for instrumental variable estimator)
Dependent Variable: SPC18

	Variable	*Value*	*SE*	*T*	*S*
LSPC18	.66397	.09171	7.23961	.005	
FD	−156.479	44.5332	−3.51377	.005	R^2=.94
ANSA	−239.004	65.1775	−3.62094	.005	S =.005
ADDEF	00000166	.00000065	2.54835	.025	DF=15
EFINX18	−229.4	72.8	−3.15213	.005	D =1.77
Constant (c)	2146.45				

Model 2.2   (Corrected for instrumental variable estimator)
Dependent Variable: SPC14

	Variable	*Value*	*SE*	*T*	*S*
LSPC14	.65502	.08751	7.48477	.005	
FD	−129.769	38.4690	−3.37334	.005	R^2=.94
ANSA	−229.370	56.0409	−4.09290	.005	S =.005
ADDEF	.00000142	.00000057	2.48629	.025	DF=15
EFINX14	−205.2	57.1	−3.60320	.005	D =1.8
Constant (c)	2063.0				

ANALYSIS OF THE RESULTS

It is well known that an "incorrect" model can often provide a good forecast for the phenomenon under investigation. On the other hand, following the philosophy of logical positivism, there is no case in which one is permitted to label a model a "true" one. Each theoretical statement is subject to verification and justification through empirical observation. While one can make a case against acceptance of the model, one cannot ignore the fact that the good fit increases the degree of confidence in it. The tests for fit, i.e., R^2 and T statistics, are more than satisfactory. The models are highly significant and ninety-four percent of the variance is explained. This result is partly due to the presence of a lagged dependent variable in the model. If the goal of the test is to provide support for a theory, then the support provided by these models is plentiful.

Before going into a detailed analysis of the models and the interpretation of the results, it will be useful to discuss the effects of the different age groups and attempt to determine which is the most relevant group for the analysis.

The results of the corrected models (2.1) for the older population and (2.2) for the younger group do not really help in answering the question of which age group should be considered in the estimation process. Both models perform well: all variables which were found to be significant in one were also significant in the other. In fact, when measurement of fit is considered, they are virtually identical (compare R^2's and T statistics). The negligible differences between them are shown only in the values of the estimators.

However, because of the fact that the correlation coefficient between these two age groups was almost unity (i.e., 0.98), the dilemma was solved by treating both models interchangeably. This is also because, in general, utilizing data that only approximate reality, one can rule out the possibility of perfectly reflecting reality. Thus, the researcher should be more concerned with the magnitude and the direction of the phenomenon than with its exact value. In this case the differences found were marginal and can legitimately be ignored.

The Effect of the Regulation on Sales

For the younger group (those fourteen and older), the Fairness Doctrine, operating for only three years (1968-1970) caused an average reduction of 130 units per capita, which is about 6.5 packages per person. The ANSA, starting in 1964, caused an average reduction of 11.5 packages annually. In 1968, there were about 145 million American residents over the age of fourteen, and in 1975 there were less than 164 million. Since the interest here lies only in the magnitude of the effect, the figure 150 million was chosen to represent the average population during those years. It is easy to see

that while the industry lost 2.7 billion packages of cigarettes between 1968 and 1970 due to the combined effect of the two variables, it lost only 1.7 billion during the five years after 1970. Considering the 1.5 cent profit margin the industry derived from each
package sold, it can be seen that while between 1968 and 1970
they lost 40.5 million dollars in profit, they lost only 25.5 million
after 1970.

This is, of course, a literal interpretation of the findings, which
provides only part of the picture. Although these results are already compatible with the argument that the industry was better
off after the ban, it will be shown now that it is indeed in a much
better position than indicated by the relative reduction of these
losses. For this purpose the analytical procedure known as the
"impact multiplier" is employed.

The multiplier effect. To explain the operation of the multiplier, the following hypothetical simple linear regression model is
used: [32]

$$Y_t = \beta_1 Y_{t-1} + \beta_2 X_{2t} + U_t$$

where X_2 denotes the policy intervention in the time series and
Y_{t-1} is a lagged dependent variable utilized as an explanatory
variable.

The effect of the exogenous variable X_{2t} on the dependent
variable is indicated not only by the value of the structural parameter β_2, since the current effects of X on Y_t may also be traced
to earlier years. That is, the effect is captured by the parameter of
Y_{t-1}. Thus, β_2 is only a partial description of the policy effects on
the dependent variable Y_t.

A more complete description of the effect of policy intervention
over the whole period of implementation and into the future is
possible if one considers the past effects of X_2 on Y_t. Since the
information about the effects of the intervention is carried over by
the coefficient of the instrumental variable Y_{t-1}, β_1 can serve as a
multiplier factor. When β_1 is considered together with β_2, their
multiplication will determine the cumulative effect of the policy on
Y_t. Thus, the policy variable X_2 may have an effect on Y even after
the policy maker decided to suspend implementation. The cumula-

tive effect after n years will be:

$$\beta_2 + (\beta_2 + \beta_2 - \beta_1) + (\beta_2 + \beta_2 - \beta_1^2) + \ldots + (\beta_2 + \beta_2 - \beta_1^{n-1})$$

$$= m$$

Where m denotes the cumulative effect of the policy variable in terms of the dependent variable.

Using the coefficients from model (2.2), one can compute the degree to which the Fairness Doctrine and the ANSA affected the consumption of cigarettes in the years of implementation. Moreover, as shown in Figure six, it can also be determined when the regulation will not cause an additional reduction in consumption (i.e., when the decreasing marginal effects of the regulation will approach zero).

FIGURE 6
The Separate and Combined Forecasted Effect of the Fairness Doctrine and the ANSA on the Reduction of Consumption of Cigarettes Calculated by the Impact Multiplier

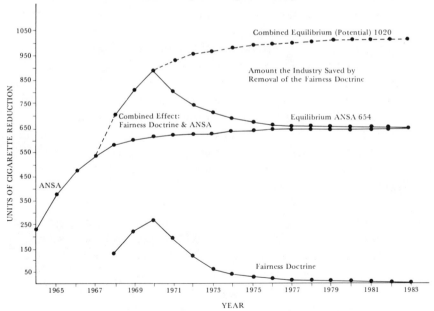

The ANSA started to affect consumption in 1964 with the publication of the Surgeon General's report. In that year, it had caused a reduction of 229 units (about 11.5 packages) in the per capita consumption of cigarettes for the population over fourteen years of age. By 1968, it had already effected a per capita reduction of 578 cigarettes — twenty-three packages — or 4.3 billion packages for the entire population of those fourteen and older. Between 1968 and 1975 (the last year of observation) all the antismoking activities apart from the Fairness Doctrine caused an additional decrease in consumption of about seventy-two units of cigarettes (3.6 packages). But by 1977, most of the additional damage to industry sales caused by the ANSA had ended, as only two units per capita were lost. By 1983 the negative effect on consumption is predicted to approach zero.

In 1968, the year the Fairness Doctrine was implemented, it caused the industry a loss of 129 units of cigarettes (6.5 packages) per capita (population of those fourteen and older). By 1970, its negative effect had already caused a reduction of 267 cigarettes (13.3 packages, or almost two billion packages for the entire population). However, once the Fairness Doctrine was removed in 1971, its potential negative effects were dissipated. After 1970, there is no longer a carried-over effect for the Fairness Doctrine, as in the case of the ANSA. Its impact is not cumulative but rather vanishing (that is, it decays exponentially from the level reached in 1970). Thus, in 1971, the Fairness Doctrine still caused a reduction in per capita consumption of 173 units of cigarettes (8.6 packages), but in 1975 this figure amounted to only a little over 1.5 packages. The negative effects of the Fairness Doctrine are predicted to vanish altogether sometime in the mid 1980s.

Clearly, the years 1968 to 1970 constitute the period when the antismoking forces scored most of their gains with respect to their goal — reduction of cigarette consumption. As seen in Figure six, the combined negative effect of the two variables was at its peak in 1970, when together they caused a reduction of about forty-five packages per capita. But the removal of the Fairness Doctrine can be considered, as explained in Chapter three, a victory for the industry. If the Fairness Doctrine was not removed at the beginning of 1971, it would have cost the industry an additional loss of forty-six cigarettes per capita, (that is, an additional loss of over five million dollars in net profit for that year alone). Had it continued further into the future, the total negative effect of the Fairness Doctrine and the ANSA is predicted to reach a peak equilibrium of over 1020 units, or fifty-one packages of cigarettes, by the year 1980 and to stabilize at that level thereafter.

The gains for the industry are, of course, indicated by the difference between the potential combined equilibrium of the Fairness Doctrine and the ANSA (i.e., 1020) and the equilibrium point the ANSA will reach in the 1980s (i.e., 654), a difference of 366 cigarettes or over eighteen packages per capita. On the other hand, a total victory for the industry over the whole regulatory process cannot be claimed. The combination of antismoking episodes seems to have had a detrimental impact on cigarette consumption. In fact, as suggested in the graph, this effect will stabilize at about thirty-three packages in a matter of five to seven years.

From the graph one can also discern the great initial effect that the Surgeon General's report had on sales, and although this was reduced in the following years, the introduction of the Fairness Doctrine resparked the negative effects of the regulation on consumption. This, with the preceding analysis, suggests that to cause substantial changes in the pattern of cigarette consumption, the public must be "shocked", by a high-intensity antismoking campaign. The initial years following the introduction of a new regulation or the transfer of negative information is the period characterized by the most substantial decrease in consumption. It is thus reasonable to expect that a campaign which increases the public awareness of the smoking-and-health issue will probably also reduce cigarette consumption.

Increasing the saliency of the issue will presumably "force" many smokers to make frequent cognitive decisions concerning their smoking behavior, but more important, it has been suggested that such campaigns, using fear as a deterent component, will be more likely to prevent non-smokers or potential smokers (i.e., youth) from taking up the habit.[33]

If an intensive antismoking campaign will not increase the impact of the health-and-smoking issue, then the antismoking forces cannot expect future gains similar to those achieved in the 1960s.

The Effective Price Index

The Effective Price Index variable appears to have a significant negative effect on consumption. The negative effect is due to the inclusion of price as one component of the index. Thus, the higher the value of the index, the lower the level of consumption will be. Since it was argued that for this specific policy issue (smoking and health) the level of disposable income should be considered a given, the policy maker who wishes to affect consumption may do so only by manipulating the price component of the index.

For the younger population model (2.2) we asked the question: What will be the effect on sales if we increase the index by one percent?

It is readily seen from model (2.2) that a one percent increase in the value of the index will amount to a decrease in the per capita consumption of cigarettes by about 205 units. This is a reduction of over ten packages on an annual basis. In 1975 there were over 213 million residents in the United States; 146.8 million were eighteen years old and older and about 163.8 million were fourteen years old and older. To determine the magnitude of the effects of the index, the figure 160 million is chosen to represent the younger population in 1975. Thus an increase of one percent in the value of the index will cause a decrease of $10.26 \times (160 \times 10^6) = 1.64$ billion packages (all other factors remain the same). Total consumption of cigarettes in 1975 was about 594 billion units (leading brands only), which when rounded up amounted to thirty billion packages. Thus, a one percent increase in the index causes an average reduction of about five percent of total sales.

The average resident (fourteen years of age and older) smoked about 187.5 packages in 1975, paying on the average (weighted across states) forty-five cents per package (undeflated). The policy maker can ask what the price of cigarettes should be, given the level of 1975 disposable income, in order for the index, with no change in other independent variables, to cause the elimination of consumption. Although this objective may be unrealistic, it nevertheless provides information about the "upper bound" for affecting consumption by price manipulation.[34] To achieve this goal, the price of a package should be nine dollars, an increase of two thousand percent over the current price!

Our hypothetical policy maker is usually more realistic. If he cannot expect to maximize his goal (i.e., eliminating consumption by price manipulation), he then attempts to cause a "satisficing" reduction in consumption.[35] He may thus wish to affect consumption in an incremental way.[36] That is, he can effect a one percent increase in the level of the index, thus reducing the level of consumption by an additional five percent. His decision to affect consumption in an incremental way may also be grounded in the fact that only part of the price component can be manipulated. The industry has no interest in contributing to a price increase. The states, because of non-uniformity in tax policies, may also have little incentive to support non-incremental increases. (As a matter of fact, due to the legal problems caused by people shopping in neighboring states and by organized bootlegging of cigarettes, some states are proposing to *reduce* their cigarette taxes.)[37] The federal decision maker is thus left with the option of increasing only that component under his control (i.e., federal tax) if he wishes to increase the level of the index by one percent.

Federal tax on cigarettes in 1975 was eight cents per package (or about four cents in 1952 prices). In order to increase the level of the index by one percent, thereby making cigarettes twice as expensive, the federal tax would have to increase from eight cents to fifty-three cents, or about 550 percent. The revenues from such an increase would rise from about 2.4 billion dollars in 1975 prices (at eight cents) to almost 13 billion dollars — a sizable gain indeed!

Whether or not this increase is feasible is open for debate. The industry would suffer a ten percent reduction of sales. This may appear to be an attractive alternative; however it contains one major flaw. A decrease of ten percent in the level of consumption does not necessarily imply that ten percent *more* people will have stopped smoking. Some may, but others may simply cut the number of cigarettes smoked per day and compensate by smoking more of each cigarette. Studies which attempted to measure how different smoking habits expose the lungs to different dosages of smoke revealed that the British often smoke their cigarettes right down to the very end. This is probably because cigarettes are heavily taxed and therefore expensive in England. In comparison to Great Britain, Canada, or Switzerland, where the price of cigarettes is considerably higher than in the United States, the U.S. smoker smokes the least of his cigarette. Americans leave the longest butts (31.4 mm), as compared with 18.7 mm in Britain, 27.9 mm in Canada, and 24.6 mm in Switzerland.[38]

The inference is that the American smoker behaves in a "safer" way while consuming the product. This point is summarized best by Simon.

> . . . if a nation wishes to decrease cigarette consumption, raising the tax on cigarettes is an obvious alternative or additional measure that might be taken. Fewer cigarettes will be bought if the price is higher . . . . However, if the price of cigarettes goes up, people will smoke the butts closer to the end, and the more of a cigarette that is smoked, the more dangerous it rapidly becomes, so an increase in taxation may not be a good alternative solution.[39]

Taxation strategies may not be a good solution when the goal of the policy maker is to reduce consumption and thus lower the health risks involved. However, reforming the existing tax structure seems desirable. More specifically, it is suggested that taxes be unified and levied at the federal level alone, thereby also reducing individual or organized violations of the law. Of course, such reform would also necessitate the establishment of a "revenue sharing" system, such that the states would receive that portion of the revenues generated by the tax on the number of cigarette packages sold in each state.

Is this proposed reform politically feasible? The answer cannot be definitive. New York state or Massachusetts may gain from such a proposal, but North Carolina and New Hampshire may not. In addition, concentrating taxation at the federal level would appear to create an ideal "single pressure point," such that the ability of the federal decision maker to increase taxes in the future may be quite limited. The reason for this will be discussed in more detail in the last chapter. At this point one may simply note that in the last three decades, there were no increases in the nominal level of federal taxes on cigarettes, and in real terms, there was a *reduction* of over fifty percent in this level if one compares federal taxation in the 1970s with the level in the 1950s.

The Effect of Advertising on Sales

Advertising, the non-manipulable variable as far as the policy maker is concerned, seems to affect sales significantly, as shown in model (2.2). However, in comparison to the performance of other variables, the effect on sales appears relatively weaker when only the values as they appear in model (2.2) are observed. It should also be noted that the small value of the parameter estimator for advertising in model (2.2), i.e., 1.42×10^{-6} may be perceptually deceiving. This value indicates that one million dollars invested in advertising increases per capita annual sales by 1.42 units. If one multiplies this figure by the number of U.S. residents (fourteen years of age and older) in 1975 (i.e., 160 million), one can see that one million dollars invested in advertising brought additional sales of about 227 million units (i.e., 11.36 million packages) for the entire relevant population.

Obviously, this result indicates two things: (a) the more spent on advertising, the more additional sales are generated; and (b) the smaller the population, the smaller the resulting gain. Since result (a) seems to contradict the argument advanced in Chapter three, that the *prime* objective of advertising in a mature oligopolistic market is to capture share of the market and not necessarily expand the market, this contradiction requires further analysis.

Recall that the industry goal was assumed to be profit maximization. If advertising is considered an investment strategy, it must yield returns that will be equal at the margin to the invested cost.[40] The 11.36 million packages sold will generate returns (at 1.5 cents profit per package) of about 170,400 dollars or 17.4 percent of the one million dollars invested. This means that for every dollar invested, the return will be seventeen cents. Alternatively, six dollars must be spent in order to get one dollar back. This hardly seems to be profit maximization. In order to break even, the industry must make a profit of ten cents per package — a figure which Bass and Horsky considered to be the lower boundary of the profit per carton! In this light, given that advertising appears to be an expensive and unreasonable venture, why then do firms advertise their products?

In the following statement an opponent of smoking addresses this question:

> The matter does not turn upon the precise extent of the impact of cigarette commercials. Millions are spent, year after year, to promote cigarettes. No one will seriously argue that these expenditures are to no significant purpose.[41]

It has already been suggested that the significant purpose of advertising in the cigarette industry is competition over market share. Several students of marketing have tried to support the hypothesis of market share response to advertising. Some have formulated and tested models with data concerning sales and advertising of cigarettes. Studies of market response to advertising should concentrate on the analysis of various brands of cigarettes and not on the firm or the aggregate industry level. For the market share hypothesis, the question that should be asked is, How well does the brand fare, given a certain amount of advertising? The question should be worded in this way because one advertised brand may be competing with another advertised brand of the same firm.

Schmalensee thoroughly examined the cigarette industry from this point of view. Although he establishes a general theorem for market share in terms of brand, he studied the six major companies rather than specific brands.[42] In a recent study Horsky examined the effectiveness of advertising in terms of market share and dollar gains. He found that of the twelve leading brands only three (Pall Mall, Tareyton, and Kool) did not gain on their invested advertising dollars between 1952 and 1970. The rest, with Brown and Williamson's Raleigh leading the group, trailed by Camel, Winston (both Reynolds) and Marlboro (Philip Morris), had drawn substantial returns from their advertising investment. Horsky thus concluded that for the twelve most successful brands, the total advertising contribution of each dollar invested in advertising is 1.60 dollars.[43] This value is very close to the figure arrived at by Peles (1.70 dollars).[44] The average total return on investment was found to be fifty percent. Clearly, then, it is quite rational for a firm to invest in advertising.

**TABLE G. Cost of Cigarette Advertising of Twelve Leading Brands,
1954-1963, 1964-1970, 1971-1975**
(in cents per carton)

Brand	Company	1954-1963	1964-1970	1971-1975
Winston	Reynolds	5.5	6.6	5.4
Pall Mall	American	3.5	5.7	5.5
Marlboro	Philip Morris	7.8	9.1	6.5
Salem	Reynolds	11.0	9.2	7.5
Kool	Brown & Williamson	5.3	8.7	3.1
Camel	Reynolds	2.6	4.6	5.6
Kent	Lorillard	6.8	10.2	9.8
Tareyton	American	9.4	13.9	7.4
Viceroy	Brown & Williamson	7.5	11.4	11.9
Raleigh	Brown & Williamson	5.7	5.8	9.2
L&M	Liggett & Myers	10.0	12.4	11.7
Lucky Strike	American	2.9	5.4	3.6

Table G presents the twelve most successful brands over the entire period surveyed, as ranked by *Advertising Age* and the Horsky study mentioned before. The table is a comparison of undeflated advertising costs per carton. It also helps compare the average annual expenditures in the three time periods delineated — before the Surgeon General's report; from the report up to the ban; and after the ban.

From this table it can be seen that indeed the twelve leaders fared well after the ban, with only Viceroy, Camel, and Raleigh spending nominally more on advertising, probably due to the additional expenditures required for launching the new filter types of these brands. One can also see that with the exception of Salem, more money was spent in the second period on all brands. If the figures from the table seem moderate, the less successful brands change the picture, especially when the second period is considered.[45] However, some of these brands may make it to the top in terms of market share.

"Market share" is a more refined concept than total size. It means a breakdown of the products into various categories (filter, non-filter, longs, standard, menthol, medium tar, etc.) Bill Hobbs, chairman of R. J. Reynolds Tobacco Company has stated,"We want a brand in every growing potential cigarette category."[46] The people in Philip Morris felt that although a certain category of brands may be less successful "it would have been irresponsible to stay out of the market and not get our chunk."[47]

Industry strategy is designed to capture market share. Reynolds, the largest company, defines a successful brand as one which wins at least 0.4 percent of the national market, a minimum required for maintaining nationwide distribution. A one percent gain in market share in the 1970s is worth fifty million dollars in added sales volume, net of federal excise taxes.[48] Reynolds recently announced, in May 1977, that it is planning to spend forty million dollars on a new low-tar introduction, "the largest sum ever spent on a single brand." The goal is to gain one percent of the market and the company expects to recover its investment in thirty-three months.[49] But this high-cost strategy should be expected to stimulate a counter-move, and in fact Brown and Williamson announced in June 1977 that they will spend fifty million dollars on its new low-tar offering "Kool Super Lights."[50]

These examples demonstrate not only that the "only game in town is market share" but also that the industry is once again entering competitive equilibrium. The reasons for this renewed aggressiveness will be discussed in the last chapter.

Finally, consider the following statement issued a few months after the ban by a top executive of Philip Morris, Frank Saunders:

> The reduction in spending is even greater than it looks, when you consider that the advertising dollar does not go as far in print media as it does in television. . . . TV advertising was never designed to create new smokers, its main purpose was to switch people from one brand to another so it is not surprising that the total sales are still rising.[51]

This statement, made by one who is actively involved, perhaps best summarizes the essence of the argument advanced in the preceding analysis.

SUMMARY

The analysis in this chapter may be summed up as follows. From 1964, when the Surgeon General's report was first released, and until 1971, when the ban was imposed on cigarette advertising in the broadcast media, antismoking regulation had the desired negative impact on sales. The 1971 ban did not impair the ability of the industry to promote its product, since advertising serves as a competitive tool used by firms to increase their share of the existing market. The suppression of this competition by the ban was beneficial to the industry. In addition, and perhaps of more importance to the industry, the ban amounted to the removal of the Fairness Doctrine, which had the unanticipated consequence of decreasing the effectiveness of the government's antismoking activities.

In the absence of other significant regulatory activities aimed at disseminating negative messages, increasing the awareness of the smoking-and-health connection, and/or increasing prices, it will be very difficult to obtain gains similar to those achieved by the antismoking forces during the 1960s.

FIVE

Conclusion and Policy Implications

FIVE

"There have been, in general," writes James Q. Wilson, "two main theories of the political causes of regulation." The first he called the public interest theory, whereby legislators are motivated by growing social demand or dramatic crisis to undertake a preventive (or protective) regulatory act. The second theory "is that regulation results when the industry successfully uses its political influence to obtain legal protection for itself or impose legal burdens on its rivals."[1] This is the self-interest theory of regulation. In the cigarette case, while the regulatory initiatives were based on the first theory, the practical consequences of them support the validity of the self-interest theory.

By July 1964, seven months after the release of the Surgeon General's report, two opposing coalitions were engaged in conflict: the National Emergency Council on Smoking and Health (the anti-smoking coalition) and the Tobacco Institute. It is of some interest to identify the members of each coalition. Ten years later the following partners were included in the health coalition: the American Academy of Pediatrics; the American Association of Health, Physical Education and Recreation; the American Cancer Society; the American College of Chest Physicians; the American College Health Association; the American College of Physicians; the American College of Radiology; the American College of Surgeons; the American Dental Association; the American Heart Association; the American Nurse's Association; the American Pharmaceutical Association; the American Public Health Association; the American School Health Association; the Association of State and Territorial Health Officials; Boy's Clubs of America; the National Board of Young Women's Christian Associations; the National Congress of Parents and Teachers; the National League for Nursing; the National Jogging Association; the National Student Nurse's Association; the National Medical Association; the Public Health Cancer Association of America; the Student American Medical Association; the National Foundation; U.S. Children's Bureau; U.S. Office of Child Development; Department of

Defense; U.S. Public Health Service; U.S. Veterans Administration; U.S. Office of Education.[2] Also in the health coalition, we can include ASH (Action on Smoking and Health), the group that was established in 1968 by John F. Banzhaf III in order to monitor the broadcast time given to the antismoking forces under the Fairness Doctrine. The two regulatory commissions (FTC and FCC) and some prominent congressmen, such as Robert and Edward Kennedy, Frank Moss, Warren Magnuson and others, were allied with this coalition.

The Tobacco Institute coalition was considerably smaller. It included the paid representatives of tobacco growers; marketing organizations and cigarette manufacturers; congressmen representing tobacco constituencies; the leading members of four subcommittees in Congress (two appropriations subcommittees and two substantive legislative committees, one in each house); and certain officials within the Department of Agriculture who were involved with the various tobacco programs of that department. This was a small, cohesive and knowledgeable group, well versed in all aspects of the tobacco industry and its relationship with the government.[3]

The joint objective of the tobacco coalition was to protect the interests of the industry against regulation that would endanger its economic well-being. They further endeavored to ensure the design of a regulation that would improve the industry's market position. As has been assumed throughout this study, the specific objective of the industry is profit maximization. Other members, however, may have participated in the coalition for different reasons. Thus, for example, the interest of southern congressmen may have been reelection to their representative positions, a goal which would be easier to obtain if they were supported by the tobacco companies, thereby guaranteeing jobs to their constituents.[4] With the vast resources available to the tobacco coalition, resources which far surpassed the two million dollars in public funds assigned to the health coalition in 1965, this group was able to generate congressional support for the design of a regulation compatible with their interests.[5]

The health coalition was hindered in other ways. As Olson points out, the extended size of the coalition worked against it — "the larger the group the less it will further its common interest."[6] In addition, their goals and incentives were loosely formulated. Chapter three addressed the question of why organizations which purport to speak in the name of the public often find themselves at a disadvantage when regulations are on an official agenda. This is because in order to represent a group as diverse as the "public," such organizations must either state their position in highly generalized terms or lose their representativeness. In addition, the nature of what they are pursuing, i.e., health, can be considered an "inclusive" goal; if other organizations and individuals express their desire to participate in the endeavor to improve health, the framers of the coalition cannot exclude them without damaging their public image and risking future support. In such cases, the size of the coalition tends to grow, and payoffs from potential "victory" must be shared among more partners.[7] As a result, the motivations and incentives of the many members of the coalition to achieve a basic solution may be weak. They may be satisfied instead with interim achievements.

It is hardly surprising, then, that the antismoking coalition succeeded to the degree that it did. This success will be evaluated using the guidelines of the four major policy questions set forth in the introduction to this study. Since Fritschler thoroughly covered the 1965 cigarette labelling act, and since his conclusion is consistent with the argument presented here, the focus of this discussion will be the 1971 prohibition.

WHO REALLY BENEFITS FROM THE REGULATION?

Benefits and costs are often very difficult to identify. What benefits did the health coalition derive from opposing smoking? Kenneth Friedman suggests "rectitude, status. . . . "[8] One might add recognition, visibility and expansion of organizational activity. Simply stated, the desired benefit to the cigarette industry, and to the principal members of the tobacco coalition, is more profit. A market situation which is not stable and which involves a high degree of uncertainty with respect to consumer behavior and/or marketing actions taken by the firms, may not contribute to the acquisition of more profit. Hence it is in the interest of the industry to turn things around by reducing the level of uncertainty and attempting to stabilize the market.

In Chapter three it was argued that the prohibition imposed on the advertising of cigarettes in the broadcasting media in effect improved the market situation for the industry. This is consistent with the view expressed by James Wilson who suggested that an organized group (like the Tobacco Institute) may receive all the benefits while the costs of the regulation will be diffused among the many members of society. In this type of situation the group can often make substantial gains by imposing constraints on the regulatory body. The constraints are carefully formulated to conform with the following characteristics:[9]

1. Price competiton within the affected industry will be eliminated or reduced.
2. Entry to the industry will be restricted or at least made more expensive.
3. The beneficiary group will strongly influence the regulatory agency that administers the policy.
4. The industry will strive to maintain a position of low visibility.

These characteristics do, in fact, manifest themselves in the tobacco case. The question to be asked then is: in what ways did the industry benefit from the regulation? Since the industry is assumed to be a profit maximizer, benefits to the industry should be assessed in terms of the comparison between the profit gained before and after the 1971 ban on advertising. The industry gained from the 1971 prohibition on advertising in the following ways:

1. The ban on advertising made the Fairness Doctrine inapplicable.
2. The industry saved money after the ban due to reduced advertising expenditures.
3. Sales (total as well as per capita) increased substantially after the ban.
4. By banning advertising in the broadcasting media, the six major firms acquired an almost lasting control of the market. Today this control amounts to over ninety-nine percent of the market. Without national advertising, it becomes very difficult for new firms to enter the market.

5. The industry still has the print media which enables it to respond, although less effectively, to alterations in consumer taste.

Of crucial importance is the determination of how well the industry improved its market position relative to itself and relative to other industries in the market. This is not a policy question, since the policy maker is not necessarily concerned with profit but rather with reducing the level of consumption and thus minimizing the risks of smoking. Profit is important, however, from a managerial point of view. A firm without present or anticipated profit may choose to leave the market, thereby satisfying the policy maker's objective.

Even prior to the implementation of the Fairness Doctrine it was remarked:

Never before has an industry spent so much money trying to talk itself out of business; the commercials keep reminding us that tobacco contains tars, resins, and other bronchial abrasives. Smokers are quite obviously committing slow suicide, but each brand claims that its own product is somewhat less lethal than other brands.[10]

In 1968, before the regulatory agencies and Congress took steps against the advertising activities of the industry, the research department of Smith, Barney and Co., member of the New York Stock Exchange, sent its customers "an investment appraisal discussing the significance of a possible ban of advertising on television and radio." The appraisal stated that

in spite of 225 million dollars spent yearly on advertising cigarettes via television and radio, domestic per capita consumption of cigarettes has declined modestly. There seems to be, furthermore, some incentive for the cigarette industry voluntarily to discontinue radio and television commercials. It may lessen the pressures on Congress for more stringent antismoking measures, and may end antismoking messages themselves. It would, on the other hand, free large sums of money to support acquisitions and diversification, utilize other forms of promotion or increase earnings.[11]

Had the ban taken place in 1968, the increase in that year's earnings per share would have been as shown in Table H.

Although the industry could not voluntarily discontinue its cigarette commercials, when they were "forced" to stop advertising in the broadcasting media their market situation improved dramatically. In the 1960s they were low in the ranking of profitable American industries.[12] In the 1970s they catapulted to the top.[13] It is not surprising, therefore, to discover the wide range of industry diversification, especially after the ban, as shown in Table I.

Does the public benefit from the regulation? The answer to this question is elusive. Clearly, the antismoking campaign was amongst the principle causes of the appearance of new brands of cigarettes emphasizing low-tar-and-nicotine content. Also, most cigarettes sold today are of the filter type, indicating a consumer concern for minimizing the threat to health.

Aware of this trend, the industry concentrated its advertising budget on the "less risky" brands. Consequently, the market share of the low-tar (fifteen milligrams and under) and low-nicotine brands increased from less than one percent in the late 1960s to 10.9 percent in 1975 and 15.8 percent in 1976.[14] The low-tar-and-nicotine cigarettes contained less than fifty percent as much tobacco as the regular filter brands, constituting an additional incentive to promote such brands.[15]

TABLE H. **Estimated Gains per Share of Common Stock in 1968 With and Without Ban on Cigarette Commercials**

Company	Earnings per Share	
	Without Ban	*With Ban*
American Tobacco	$ 3.15	$ 4.07
Liggett and Myers	2.98	4.76
Lorillard	4.67	7.41
Philip Morris	3.94	5.77
R. J. Reynolds	3.73	4.63

Source: Based on the calculations in Smith, Barney and Co., *The Cigarette Industry*, Topical Research Comment, no. 97-69, N.Y., December 1968, pp. 1-2; the figures for Brown and Williamson, a division of British American Tobacco, are not available since they are not members of U.S. stock exchanges.

TABLE I. The Range of the Cigarette Industry's Economic Diversification

Company/Category	Food (Human and Pet)	Alcohol	Manufacturing and Services	Others and Comments
American	Sunshine Biscuits Duffy-Mott (apple sauce, prune juice)	Bean Dist. Co. (bourbon)	Master Lock Co. Acme Visible Records Swingline Inc. W. R. Case & Son, Inc. Andrew Jergens Co.	
Brown & Williamson	Vita Food Products Aleutian King Crab		Kohl Corp. (supermarkets) Gimbel Bro. (department store chain)	
Liggett & Myers	Allen Products (Alpo) Perk Foods (Vets) National Oats	Paddington Corp. Carillon Import Austin, Nichols & Co. (whiskey)	Mercury Mills (rugs) Brite Industries	
P. Lorillard	Golden Nugget Co. Reed Candy			The only cigarette company acquired by an outsider, i.e., Loew's Corp.
Philip Morris	Clark Gum Co.	Miller Brewing Co.	American Safety Razor ASR Medical Ind. Wilokin (chemical); Transvision (visual aids); Burma-Vita (shaving); Milprint (packaging); Koch (textile); Nicholet Paper; Mission Viejo (real estate)	
R. J. Reynolds	Penick & Fork (My-T-Fine) The Chung King Corp. Filler Products		Filmco McLean Ind. United States Lines	American Independent Oil Co.

Source: The information in the table is generalized and only indicative of the range of
diversification. It was taken from K. Friedman, *Public Policy and the Smoking-
Health Controversy* (Lexington, Mass.: Lexington Books, 1975), pp. 35-36.
For more detailed information on the product's level see the various publications
of *LNA*, cited in note 22 to Chapter four, this text.

However, recent findings of tests performed in laboratories of
Foster D. Snell reveal that (a) almost all the leading filter brands
tested produced more poison gases (especially carbon monoxide
than the non-filter cigarettes tested; and (b) some of the new low tar
and nicotine filter cigarettes produced more nitrogen oxides than
some leading filter or non-filter brands.[16]

Since these cigarettes are more profitable to the industry, "you
wind up spending more, smoking more and getting a more dangerous
combustion for the same nicotine payoffs as stronger cigarettes."
Worse yet, it is probably a good guess that the low tar brands are
hooking millions of teenagers.

[In the past] . . .   that first Camel or Lucky made so many
kids sick that they stayed off cigarettes for good. Now so many

brands are so weak that the kids don't get sick enough to stop right away. They just get hooked.[17]

In light of these findings, it can be concluded that the industry was not harmed by the regulation and, in fact, expects sizable present and future returns. The public, on the other hand, seems to bear much of the cost of the regulation.

ARE THE REGULATIONS EFFECTIVE?

The effectiveness of a public act must be evaluated against its objectives and the resulting social costs and benefits. The ban did not reduce cigarette consumption. One can thus see the irony of Julian Simon's study, cited by John E. Moss (D-California), which predicted that cigarette smoking would drop five percent in the first "commercial free" year and would result in "an increase of human life in the United States of about 180 billion minutes or 340,000 years of life."[18]

Moreover, by banning advertising the government set up an effective barrier against market entries, which is incompatible with free competition.[19] This argument may also be extended to the brand level. In this view it becomes very difficult for a firm to successfully launch a new introduction. Hence one would expect increases in advertising outlays for new introductions in future years.

An additional side effect of the ban and the antismoking campaign was a switch to tobacco substitutes. During the years of the Fairness Doctrine, when cigarette consumption was declining, sales of cigars and smoking and chewing tobacco were booming. According to *Business Week* (June 20, 1970, p. 32), consumption of chewing and smoking tobacco between 1968 and 1970 increased by about thirteen million pounds, from 137 to about 150 million pounds. The figures for cigars showed similar increases. It is generally assumed that non-cigarette tobacco products are "safer," either because they are made of pure tobacco leaves or due to the fact that people do not usually inhale the smoke. The closest substitute for cigarettes are little cigars. Table J demonstrates the increased consumption of this product, showing a steady upward trend.

TABLE J. Little Cigars Sold in the U.S. Between the Years 1967 and 1973
(in million units)

Year	1967	1968	1969	1970	1971	1972	1973
Quantity	430.7	503.7	731.0	894.4	1080.4	3932	4337

Source: Figures for 1967-1971 are from *Advertising Age*, July 10, 1972, p. 52; for 1972-1973, September 16, 1974, p. 8. The total consumption of cigars (large and small) between 1970 and 1973 was as follows, in millions of pounds: 1970 (7979), 1971 (7868), 1972 (8009), 1973 (11,422). See *Statistical Abstract*, 1975, table no. 1270, p. 751.

Consider now the information with regard to little cigars after 1973. While in 1973, 4,337 million little cigars were sold, in 1974, only 3,067 million units were sold, and in 1975 even fewer — 2,897.[20] What happened in 1973 that led to this dramatic decrease? In January 1973, the FTC recommended that little cigar radio and television advertising be prohibited. On September 10 of that year Congress passed legislation extending the prohibition to include this product.[21] Thus, the regulation did effectively prevent the industry from luring smokers to a safer substitute. This also implies further restriction of competition (in this case across markets).

The failure of the prohibition on cigarette commercials was realized by Bruce W. Wilson, Deputy Assistant Attorney General, who said in a Senate Consumer Subcommittee hearing in February 1972 that

> the public interest might be better served through the resumption of both cigarette commercials and the antismoking messages that were so prevalent before the broadcasting ban.[22]

Another observer who realized the failure of the ban is the outspoken Nicholas von Hoffman who writes:

> While the cigarette industry was making a perfectly splendid transition from broadcasting back to print . . . the antismoking forces were failing to make a successful adjustment to the new condition. The FTC is bogged down with such projects as trying

to make the cigarette industry enlarge the health hazard sign on
the billboards . . . .[23]

Von Hoffman proposes that

a new attack is necessary . . . to begin with we might let the
cigarette makers back on TV and then once we've got them back
on the air, let's fight it out with them for the lives and health of
their consumers.[24]

Perhaps such thinking motivated people like Bruce McGorrill, a
manager of a Kansas City television station, to campaign for the
resumption of cigarette commercials, but only for low-tar-and-
nicotine brands — "in the same manner that beer and wine are
allowed and hard liquor is prohibited."[25] Unfortunately, it seems
that the antismoking forces, although aware of the "shortcomings"
of the ban, have not learned much from their experience.[26] In dis-
closing their future strategy, the American Cancer Society hoped,
among other things, to "initiate, immediately, activity to bring
about congressional action to ban advertising of cigarettes in the
next five years . . . ."[27] The possible implications of this unlikely
regulation will be discussed later.

WHAT ARE THE ROLES OF INFORMATION AND POLITICS IN THE FORMULATION AND IMPLEMENTATION OF REGULATION?

There were, and still are, several misconceptions regarding smoking
and related matters. This study has attempted to examine certain
issues, but others require further investigation. For instance, on the
basis of what knowledge did each side formulate its strategy?

The cigarette industry was aware that advertising is most effective as a tool for competing over market shares. The statistical test
presented in Chapter four supports this position. It follows that the
restriction of advertising primarily affects the degree of competition
among firms within the industry. On the other hand, the antismoking
forces did not successfully manipulate their single most effective
tool, the Fairness Doctrine. Either they were unaware of its efficacy,
or they were willing to trade it for the ban and the semblance of
victory.

The American Cancer Society, one of the more important members of the health coalition, admits that it simply overlooked the fact that imposition of the ban would also result in the removal of the Fairness Doctrine:

> While this law [the prohibition on advertising act] was hailed as a victory for the antismoking forces, *it could not be foreseen* that it would also produce a serious drawback. Since the broadcasters could no longer advertise cigarettes, they no longer were required to carry anticigarette messages. How powerful these messages had really been was demonstrated by what happened when they were no longer there. By the end of 1971, the per capita consumption curve for cigarettes had begun to point upward again; then it continued to move up gradually through 1972, 1973 and 1974.[28]

In Chapter two it was pointed out that John Mueller had foreseen exactly this. If there were any doubts that the Fairness Doctrine was an effective means for influencing people to reduce consumption, they could no longer have existed after the explicit statement made by Irving Rimer, vice president of public information for the American Cancer Society, who announced in 1977 that "antismoking advertising works."[29]

From this, it may seem that members of the health coalition were simply not aware of the consequences of prohibiting the advertising of cigarettes. Yet since it is possible that they were aware that they might lose control of the effective tool of the Fairness Doctrine, the question should be asked: Why did they agree to this trade-off? The answer is not clear. It is possible that being involved in a coalition, one or several elements within the coalition (i.e., the regulatory agencies) saw the possibility of scoring a victory in the episodic conflict, specifically in the arena where they had the legal responsibility of regulating the industry. Thus, the FTC and the FCC directed the attention of the public and the health coalition toward the role of advertising in promoting the consumption of cigarettes. As shown in Appendix A, the FCC issued a notice of the proposed regulation to ban advertising at the beginning of 1969. The objective of the prohibition, as expressed by Senator Moss, was aimed

> mainly . . . at protecting young people who had not yet begun to

smoke but were subjected to powerful inducements to smoking via television advertising of cigarettes. [30]

It may also be that some members in the health coalition sincerely believed that

> sophisticated advertising techniques are often used to deceive, cajole, and exploit the youngest and least knowledgeable members of our society . . . [31]

Perhaps, then, by making advertising responsible for the life of children, it became very difficult for other members of the coalition, even if they knew the logical consequences of the ban, to oppose the thrust of the regulatory agencies toward this particular solution.

To be sure, the Tobacco Industry was clearly aware of this. They needed only to look at their sales figures. They also knew that

> advertising does not sell many cigarettes . . . and that cigarettes had reached a point of "market maturity" of products — meaning that nearly all the people who are going to buy them at a particular point in time are doing so already. All that advertising will do with such products is to influence people to use one brand in preference to another. . . . Anyone who knows anything about cigarettes and cigarette marketing also knows that cigarettes are their own best salesmen. [32]

The history of cigarette consumption in the United States and in other countries demonstrates that even in periods of no advertising cigarette consumption increases. John Maxwell, for example, as early as 1964, informed the industry that between 1921 and 1927, when the sale and advertising of cigarettes was banned in fourteen states, per capita consumption (based on the population of those fifteen years old and older) of cigarettes enjoyed its fastest rate of growth, almost doubling to 1,174 units. [33] The industry also knew that in Great Britain, where cigarette ads had already been banned from television, sales rose by about 2.7 percent annually. In Italy, the post-1962 television ban period showed an annual increase of more than 3.5 percent. France, with no television advertising of cigarettes, had an annual growth rate (after 1964) of nearly six percent. Likewise, sales in Switzerland rose eight percent without television.[34] Thus, losing the broadcasting media, especially given the fact that the opposing side concurrently lost its principal means of attacking the industry, was not unattractive after all.

Can it be that the antismoking forces were unaware of such developments? Had they not read the statistics as carefully as the industry people? Elizabeth Drew's article of May 4, 1969, in the *New York Times,* clearly indicated that the health coalition was fully aware of the fact that the prohibition regulation had been proven ineffective in other countries. Why then did they "push" a regulation of this nature? It was suggested before that they might have been forced by members of their coalition, in particular the regulatory agencies, to adopt this particular solution. In addition, a case can be made for the argument that the health coalition was maneuvered into this solution by the opposing party. The answers to these queries perhaps show that the decision was based not so much on the available information as on politics.[35]

The period immediately following the release of the Surgeon General's report witnessed a proliferation of proposals for the regulation of cigarette advertising and/or labelling, which led to disputes over whether such a regulation should be established by legislation, by administrative action, or by the industry itself. The tobacco industry's position then, as it is now, was that if any action were to be taken, prior congressional authorization was necessary. The concept behind such a position is that Congress will design a uniform policy prohibiting local action against the product and/or its marketing methods.

From January 1, 1965, the industry undertook self-imposed advertising restrictions which forbade members from showing commercials aimed at persons under the age of twenty-one. The broadcasting industry also participated in monitoring the code, controlling advertising and restricting misleading pictures of the pleasures of smoking, particularly in regard to young people. However, these self-regulatory efforts were apparently unsuccessful. In 1969, in a congressional hearing, Warren Braren, manager of the National Association of Broadcasters' (NAB) Advertising Code Authority, charged that his institution had a history of "failure in controlling cigarette commercials which appeal to young people." He also said that the strategy of the industry had been "to avoid meaningful self-regulatory action as long as the possibility exists that Congress will enact legislation favorable to the broadcasting and tobacco industry."

The industry's inability to regulate itself demonstrates that the various firms had strong incentives to break agreements in order to improve their relative market position. In 1964, the Federal Trade Commission, the independent agency which oversees product advertising, assumed that it possessed regulatory power over the labelling and advertising of cigarettes. Since cigarettes were considered to be a *product* and not a food or drug, the FDA (the Food and Drug Administration of HEW) claimed no authority in this area. But in June 1964, the Surgeon General, Dr. Luther L. Terry (also of HEW) said that the FDA could best handle the job if given a congressional mandate. When the National Clearinghouse on Smoking and Health was established in 1965, the Public Health Service (PHS) of HEW received custody over it. The FCC got its share of responsibility with the implementation of the Fairness Doctrine.

The political developments prior to and following the 1965 Labelling Act were discussed extensively by Fritschler. One clause of the act prohibited further attempts by the FTC or other regulatory agencies to restrict the advertising and marketing practices of the industry until 1969. But that did not stop the FTC from planning a comeback in 1969. On July 1, 1968, HEW and the FTC released reports linking cigarettes more firmly to diseases and calling for greater restriction of cigarette advertising. In that year, the FTC, in a three-to-two decision, voted to recommend a ban on all cigarette advertising on radio and television. Warren G. Magnuson (D-Washington), chairman of the Senate Commerce Committee and an old foe of the tobacco industry, said that the committee would give the recommendation "serious consideration." The final outcome, as we know, was the advertising ban, approved by Congress in 1969 and signed by President Nixon in 1970.

What congressional support did the industry have? In 1965, when the label regulation was discussed, virtually all southern congressional leaders, senators and representatives, rallied to support the industry, "because the regulations could affect nearly every district in the south. . . . " In addition the industry cause was embraced by the conservatives — mostly Republicans — who objected to stringent federal regulation of private industry. The importance of tobacco taxes as sources of revenue in most states influenced the positions of other members. And the potential impact of the advertising regulation on the incomes of the advertising, broadcasting and news industries, whose support was vital each election year, brought additional supporters. If this coalition was able to design an act (the Labelling Act) which most observers hailed as a victory for the industry, why did it dissipate when faced with the potentially more serious ban on advertising?

The answer was revealed in the theoretical discussion in Chapter three, where it was argued that the ban served the interest of the industry. In 1967, Gary Lessner and John Maxwell, Jr., the industry analysts, as well as other tobacco executives, realized that although the health scare did not deter *many* smokers, it made the Wall Street stockholder a little shy. As a result, tobacco company stocks fell. They also pointed out

> that the ad man knows that advertising does not make or break the cigarette market. He has seen cigarette sales increase in both England and Italy, despite the lack of television advertising.[36]

In the domestic market, the liquor industry, which does not advertise in the broadcasting media, continued to grow and successfully introduce new brands. (The tobacco companies must indeed have known this since some of them are in the liquor business as well; see Table I.) Equipped with this knowledge, Joseph F. Cullman III, chairman of the Tobacco Institute Executive Committee, in a statement to the Senate in 1969, offered to discontinue cigarette ads in the broadcasting media, at the latest by September 1970, when "major contractual arrangements" for air time will expire. Furthermore, he said that advertising could end *sooner* if the broadcasting industry would agree to cancel existing contracts simultaneously at any point after December 1969. The only condition attached to this proposition was a congressional waiver from antitrust laws since such communal withdrawal may have been considered a collusive act on the part of the manufacturers.

Through this proposal, the industry rejected an earlier plan offered by the NAB to phase out cigarette commercials gradually over a four-year period beginning on January 1, 1970. The date for termination of the ads suggested by the industry was earlier than that offered by the FTC, i.e., 1971. Interestingly enough, support for Cullman's proposal came from none other than Senator Frank E. Moss (D-Utah) the arch-opponent of the industry. Moss proposed an amendment offering a special exemption from the antitrust laws, enabling the industry to withdraw all commercials simultaneously by September 1970. The old "foe-turned-friend" argued that it was a "bad precedent for Congress to ban advertisements for a product that was not unlawful and that cigarette manufacturers should be allowed to act voluntarily." He later reversed his position in favor of an imposed ban, saying: "I think we achieve our prime objective either way."

The industry concurred with the view that the prohibition bill (HR6543) strengthened somewhat the health warning on cigarette packages and at the same time prohibited the FTC from requiring any health warning on printed cigarette advertising until on or after July 1, 1971. *It also prohibited all state and local health-related regulation or prohibition of cigarette advertising.*

In this light, it is not surprising to find out that minority views in the House were expressed against the latter provisions of the bill. For example Brock Adams (D-Washington), John D. Dingell (D-Michigan), and John Jacman (D-Oklahoma) called the House 1969 bill "sweeping carte blanche protection for a particular industry." Bob Eckhardt (D-Texas) expressed another minority view. In his opinion the bill "would cut off debate on the hazards of smoking." The anticigarette bloc in the House was never able to command more than about forty votes. Consequently ten amendments to the bill proposed by the various antismoking proponents were rejected. It is interesting to note that the debate in the House in 1969 contained no reference to advertising of cigarettes on radio and television. The bill was first accepted unanimously by a House-Senate conference on March 3, 1970, and on March 18 was adopted by voice vote. The only change required by the House was to move the date of implementation from January 1 to January 2 of that year, presumably so that the special New Year's Day telecast could include the industry's final messages.

Congress then proceeded to pass a new agricultural tobacco support plan which went into effect with the 1971 harvest.[37]

WAS THE REGULATION JUSTIFIED?

If justification of a regulation is to be found in the achievement of its stated or intended objectives, then the prohibition imposed on cigarette commercials was not justified.[38]

Justification is not only an evaluative question but also a normative one. The question that must be asked is, Given a particular market imperfection, were the regulations addressed to remedying that particular imperfection? First, the issue of what constitutes a "market imperfection" in the case of cigarettes must be established.

The market is imperfect when it fails to respond to the desires of the members of society. This is the answer provided in the vast, normative literature on "public finance." The public's expectations are not met when externalities exist in the production or consumption of a product or when the market cannot provide optimal amounts of a desired good.[39] In such cases the people appeal to the government to provide them with desired results. The existence of government intervention, by definition, creates externalities and affects the utility function of society's members. It is even more important to realize that when society prohibits child labor, or the public sale of heroin, or abortion, to mention a few examples, it is not curing a market failure but rather is restricting market fulfillment of undesirable needs.

Cigarette smoking was never salient as an election issue. Cigarettes are legal products, and as long as Congress does not choose to negate this legality, production and consumption need not be restricted. The many studies which have proved that smoking is a health hazard bring up the question of the responsibility of our elected institutions toward us, as individuals and as groups. The issue of freedom of choice is also involved here.[40] Only recently have antismoking groups tried to advance a stronger normative argument, that of the negative external effects of smoking on nonsmokers. This clearly constitutes an externality.[41] One can also find solid normative grounds for the Cigarette Labelling Act in the name of "the people's right to know." The cigarette industry's unwillingness or inability to voluntarily inform the public that its product is dangerous constitutes some justification for having imposed a label.

In most industries, the nature of competition is such that if a firm makes a misleading advertising statement, competitors have an incentive to make the public aware of the deception. In the cigarette industry,

> if one manufacturer stated or implied that smoking his cigarette was healthful it would be foolish for the others to reply that smoking was in fact hazardous. No cigarette manufacturer can correct a false claim without disparaging his own product. The more effective course would be to match the claim. . . . Nor is it the case where, once a consumer has discovered the truth, they can be expected to retaliate against the deception by switching to other sellers; no one sells a non-hazardous cigarette.[42]

Hence, there is a "reverse" free rider problem and a market imperfection. Thus the FTC was quite justified in prohibiting the industry from making any claims in its advertisements that would imply, directly or indirectly, that cigarettes are not dangerous and/or that they are associated with good health. But the fact that the agency modified its restriction in the late 1960s and allowed the firms to advertise low-tar-and-nicotine cigarettes, demanding, in an act formulated in July 1971, that cigarette advertisements contain information on only two properties of the product, certainly contradicts the logic of their former stand.

Such a requirement implies that the low-tar-and-nicotine cigarettes are safer than other brands. As was noted earlier, recent findings cast doubt on this. Furthermore, since at our present state of knowledge we do not know with certitude what directly contributes to cancer and other diseases, neither in general nor in terms of the specific content of cigarettes, a concentration on and a requirement to advertise only two properties of the product is probably enabling other imperfections to appear on the market. In this light, the proposed Hart-Kennedy legislation of 1976, which would add new taxes to cigarettes based on their tar and nicotine content, would further extend a possible myth.[43] The probability of the bill's acceptance is remote, but if it is accepted, it will lend credence to and probably increase the availability of such "safe" cigarettes in the market.[44] This partly explains the huge sums recently spent by Reynolds to promote Real and Brown and Williamson's expensive campaign for Kool Super Lights.

The Fairness Doctrine is a different matter. It has its roots in the speeches of Herbert Hoover and in the decisions of the Federal Radio Commission as early as 1929. In essence, the Fairness Doctrine requires that when a broadcaster allows his facilities to be used for presentation of one side of a controversial issue, he must see that the other viewpoint is presented as well. Under the rules which the FCC adopted in July 1967, even "commentary within a news program (such as Eric Sevareid's commentary within Walter Cronkite's CBS Evening News Program) *is still subject to the general Fairness Doctrine.*"[45]

That the Fairness Doctrine, when implemented, is effective has already been shown. That it reached people and influenced the decision of marginal smokers to quit was also determined in a survey conducted in the Florida area. There, it was reported, the commercials had their greatest effect on those who smoked the least. The heavy smoker, most often the one who had steadily built up his behavior over the years, was markedly less inclined to be affected by the communication. Among those who smoked two to three packs a day, not one reported that commercials affected him in any way.[46] Thus, just as commercials for a product reinforce consumer loyalty, antiproduct commercials reinforce the decision to quit smoking, but only those persons who were inclined to give up smoking reported that the commercials had a significant effect.[47]

It still remains unclear which market "imperfection" is remedied by the Fairness Doctrine. One might, as was mentioned, justify the Fairness Doctrine on the grounds of "the people's right to know." By 1968, almost every current and potential smoker could read the warning label and be informed that cigarette smoking is hazardous. There was, however, disagreement among statisticians and members of the medical profession about the validity of various aspects of the statistical tests which linked smoking to health. Paradoxically, the implementation of the Fairness Doctrine contributed to the public controversy. When the FCC set up the precedent of the Fairness Doctrine in 1967, it was explicitly declared that the situation with respect to cigarettes was "unique."[48] The FCC opposed arguments stating that application of the Fairness Doctrine to commercial advertising was an unwarranted and dangerous extension. They claimed that the ruling was limited to cigarettes and did not imply that "any appeal to the commission by a vocal minority will suffice to classify advertising of a product as controversial and of public importance."[49] However, the precedent was established and the court held that the principle of providing free air-time to reply on controversial issues must also be guaranteed to other commercial advertisements. Thus, in at least two cases, in 1970 (a department store) and 1971 (high-powered cars and leaded high-octane gasoline), the principle was applied.[50] Since American society is blessed with pluralism of opinions and since there is no lack of controversial issues, the continuation of such a trend and the requirement that the broadcast industry must guarantee free broadcasting time for the representation of the many opinions could mean only that this industry would suffer tremendous economic difficulties in trying to meet its obligations under the Fairness Doctrine. Consequently, the nature and quality of the information transferred to the public could suffer.[51]

It can only be repeated that the Fairness Doctrine was the single most effective method for influencing smokers to change their habits. To return to the discussion concerning the proposal previously mentioned, cigarette commercials should be reinstated and the Fairness Doctrine re-implemented. But this strategy is neither feasible nor likely. First, Congress would have to reverse its ruling. Second, the FCC would have to rule again for its implementation, a move which clearly would be challenged again in court by the tobacco industry and/or the broadcasting industry. The latter, which had already challenged this FCC ruling in the late 1960s, would stand to lose considerable income if required once again to guarantee free time to antiproduct commercials. That the cigarette industry stands to lose needs no comment, but interestingly enough on May 5, 1971, representatives of the tobacco industry argued in the U.S. Court of Appeals that since paid or unpaid antismoking commercials are aired, and since the issue is still controversial, the industry should get free time under the Fairness Doctrine to represent their side. The FCC refused and the court upheld the decision.

In terms of the theoretical discussion advanced in Chapter three, the industry's appeal makes no sense. They were in effect demanding a return to a less profitable situation. But the grounds on which the court reached its decision are extremely important. The request of the industry was denied because "a broadcaster can reasonably determine that the effect of smoking on health was *no longer* controversial" so that "the commission, therefore, was justified in reaching the conclusion that, regardless of its former views on the controversy over cigarettes, it is now reasonable for a licensee to assume that the detrimental effects of cigarette smoking on health are beyond controversy."[52] Following this decision, if cigarette commercials were again aired, there could be no legal grounds for the implementation of the Fairness Doctrine.

Finally, on what normative grounds can the ban be justified? This is a very difficult question, perhaps because there are no valid answers. Certainly the desire that "Marlboro Country will fade away into television history . . . " as expressed by Senator Moss, hardly constitutes a normative basis for regulation.[53] Advertising, inaccurate health claims, or even "gross abuses" of advertising could easily be checked on a case-by-case basis by the FTC. Section five of the FTC act of 1914, which was amended in 1938, directs the commission to prevent "unfair or deceptive acts or practices" as well as "unfair methods of competition."

How can a total advertising ban, then, serve and be justified as a remedy for unfair advertising? "Prohibitions and bans," writes Jerome Rothenberg, "are clumsy instruments, covering in a blanket fashion a very wide variety of circumstances, without regard for cost or for relative seriousness of one kind of damage as compared with another. There is no provision to ensure — or even to determine roughly — whether the overall reduction is worth the cost."[54]

A case could be made, perhaps even a strong one, for banning certain products without exact knowledge of their consequences. A likely candidate might be a product whose unknown effects could produce far-reaching damages, where failure to act immediately would only increase that *possible* damage. The cost of policing the ban is negligible compared with the possible cost which will result if indeed the damage does materialize. In this respect, the normative ground is close in spirit to the concept of our responsibility to Churchman's "future man."[55]

However, a prohibition on cigarettes was not considered a feasible alternative. Smokers are usually well informed and aware that they are risking their future. In some circumstances the "market" even takes these considerations into account. For example, some insurance companies charge their smoking customers higher rates than non-smokers.

It is up to the consumer to make a choice between smoking and quitting. The role of government should be simply to enable them to make that choice an informed and educated one. This was accomplished by the label and by the Fairness Doctrine. Banning advertising for (and in this case even against) the product does not contribute to this important educational function. Furthermore, future restriction on other media of advertising, although highly unlikely, would not be compatible with the "people's right to know" or, alternatively, with their "freedom of choice."

FINAL NOTE

Conclusions can often be banal and trite. To avoid further repetition, a forecast of the future is in order. It has been shown that at least for the short term, the industry is thriving financially. This market situation developed not in spite of public regulation but rather because of it. In the long term, future government intervention may only serve to reinforce the industry.

Intervention through taxation is most likely to prevail in the case of cigarettes. In Chapter four it was argued that the rationale for taxation policies is related less to health and more to the need for increased revenues on the part of the individual states. The smoking population thus becomes an easy target for levying taxes. It was suggested that in order to combat organized crime or the bootlegging phenomenon, a reform of the tax system should be considered. A uniform federal tax system with a "revenue sharing" mechanism appears to be a reasonable solution. The income from cigarette taxes could be redistributed to the various states in accordance with the per capita consumption of cigarettes in each state. This, or other criteria for allocating rebates to the states, may dampen their incentive to participate further in actions aimed at reducing the smoking population. Conceivably, however, even if organized crime is checked by such reform, it is very unlikely that the states will accept this solution. A bill in this spirit which was introduced in the House during the week of November 7, 1977, concedes in effect that the problem is beyond law enforcement. It would remove any incentive to bootleg by substituting for the varying state and local taxes a uniform federal tax of thirty-one cents per pack. That approach would be effective, but it was observed that "states' rights" arguments are almost certain to kill it in Congress.[56]

What can be done? To begin with, high-tax states should reduce their taxation level. This may actually increase revenues since by reducing the amount of cigarettes smuggled, taxes will be collected on more packages. Another way to combat crime is to try to influence people to consume less of the product. This will, of course, be compatible with the prime goal of the legislators, that of minimizing the risks to health generated by smoking.

Educational programs should be conducted; information should be passed on to consumers; professional social agents, such as physicians or nurses, should help convince people to stop smoking. Private organizations should be asked to restrict areas for smokers and non-smokers or to prohibit smoking in their facilities. The United States is an open society, and such activities are only fair. And inevitably, the government will be there, to observe that the conflict is indeed fairly conducted.

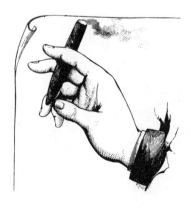

REFERENCES

Chapter One

[1] For a general discussion of public regulation with regard to utility industries and others, see Clair Wilcox, "Regulation of Industry" in David Sills (ed.), *International Encyclopedia of the Social Sciences* (New York: Macmillan, 1968), vol. 13, pp. 390-396.

Chapter Two

[1] The early days of the tobacco industry and governmental policies toward it are described by Meyer Jacobstein, *The Tobacco Industry in the United States* (New York: Columbia University Press, 1907).

[2] Cited in Vertrees J. Wyckoff, *Tobacco Regulation in Colonial Maryland* (Baltimore: Johns Hopkins Press, 1936), p. 25.

[3] See George L. Beer, *The Origins of the British Colonial System, 1578-1660* (New York: Macmillan, 1908), p. 73.

[4] Adam Smith, *The Wealth of Nations* (New York: Modern Library, 1937, first published 1776), p. 889.

[5] Other sources of tax were liquor and imports. See T. J. Woofter, *The Plight of Cigarette Tobacco* (Chapel Hill: University of North Carolina Press, 1931), p. 56.

[6] Between the first two years 1794 and 1796, the net revenue to the government from taxation was $26,961. For a discussion of the tax policies on tobacco prior to the present century see Jacobstein, *op. cit.*, pp. 185-199.

[7] See J. C. Robert, *The Story of Tobacco in America* (New York: Knopf, 1949), p. 112.

[8] U.S. Laws, Statutes, 38th Congress, 1st session, 1864, chapter 173.

[9] Those complaints were not new. In fact, in the early 1830s antitobacco societies arose throughout the United States. Between 1857 and 1872 one such society issued a publication entitled "Antitobacco Journal." See Richard B. Tennant, *The American Tobacco Industry* (New Haven: Yale University Press, 1950), p. 131. Tennant cites a gem that appeared in July 1880, in the *Harper's New Monthly Magazine* (p. 320): " 'I'll never use tobacco, no; it is a filthy weed. I will never put it in my mouth,' said Little Robert Reed. 'It hurts the health, it makes bad breath, 'tis very bad indeed. I'll never, never use it, no,' said little Robert Reed."

[10] E. Northop, *Science Looks at Smoking* (New York: Coward-McCann, 1957), p. 120.

[11] M. E. Brecher et al., Consumers' Union Report, *Licit and Illicit Drugs* (Boston: Little, Brown and Co., 1972), p. 231.

[12] New York State Constitutional Convention Committee, *Constitution of the States and the United States* (Albany: J. B. Lyon, 1938), article XVIII, section 1, pp. 10-11.

[13] Vance Packard, "USA: Cigarette Consumption Increases in spite of Restrained Advertising," *Tobacco Journal International*, August 1975, p. 263.

[14] See Reavis Cox, *Competition in the American Tobacco Industry* (New York: Columbia University Press, 1933), pp. 18-21.

[15] *United States* v. *American Tobacco Co.*, 221 U.S. 106, 186 (1911).

[16] Tennant, *op. cit.*, p. 80.

[17] See, for example, Milton Friedman, who reserved such rights for the government, in *Capitalism and Freedom* (Chicago: University of Chicago Press, 1962), p. 34.

[18] *United States Tobacco Journal*, November 1912, p. 5, cited in Cox, *op. cit.*, p. 39.

[19] The cases were *American Tobacco Co. et al.* v. *U.S.*, 147, F 2nd, 93 (1944) and 328 U.S. 781 (1946). For a discussion of these cases see William H. Nicholls, "The Tobacco Case of 1946," in the *American Economic Review* 39, no. 3, May 1949, pp. 284-296.

[20] Among the small firms the most notable are U.S. Tobacco Company, Larus and Brothers, and Stephano and Brothers.

[21] A good example of such rounding-up procedures is vending machines. The recognition that this is, and will be, the case with regard to retailers was expressed as early as 1931 by the president of Liggett and Myers, Mr. Andrew. See William H. Nicholls, *Price Policies in the Cigarette Industry* (Nashville: Vanderbilt University Press, 1951), p. 85.

[22] Lester G. Telser, "Advertising and Cigarettes," *Journal of Political Economy* 70, no. 5, October 1962, p. 476.

[23] American Cancer Society, *Task Force on Tobacco and Health, Target 5*, 1976, p. 5.

[24] See Harry M. Wootten, "In Changing Cigarette Market . . ." *Printers' Ink*, December 31, 1954, pp. 26-30.

[25]The Monopolies Commission, *Cigarette Filter Rods* (London: Her Majesty's Stationary Office, July 1969), p. 1.

[26]See "Embattled Tobacco's New Strategy," in John A. Larson (ed.), *The Regulated Businessman* (New York: Holt, Rinehart and Winston, 1966), pp. 200-201.

[27]Reported *ibid.*, pp. 119-120.

[28]John C. Maxwell Jr., "Cigarette Marketing: What's Ahead?" *Printers' Ink* February 4, 1964, p. 28.

[29]See Elizabeth B. Drew, "The Quiet Victory of the Cigarette Lobby," *Atlantic Monthly*, September 1965, p. 77.

[30]U.S. Department of Health, Education and Welfare, *Smoking and Health: Report of the Advisory Committee to the Surgeon General of the Public Health Service*, document no. 1103 (Washington, D.C.: U.S. Government Printing Office, 1964).

[31]The date-by-date actions of the FTC and the FCC were summarized by the Tobacco Institute, and appear in Appendix A.

[32]See Appendix A.

[33]Public Law 89-92, 15, U.S.C. 1331-1339. The text was changed in 1969 to a stronger version: "Warning: The Surgeon General has determined that cigarette smoking is dangerous to your health."

[34]Drew, *op. cit.*

[35]A. L. Fritschler, *Smoking and Politics: Policy Making and the Federal Bureaucracy* (New York: Meredith Corporation, 1969), p. 112.

[36]This is the position held by the American Cancer Society. See *op. cit.*, p. 7.

[37]Communications Act, 315 (a), 47 U.S.C.

[38]Christopher Lydon, "Ban on TV Cigarette Ads Could Halt Free Spots against Smoking," *New York Times*, August 16, 1970. There exists much disagreement as to what is the closest approximation. J. C. Hamilton estimated seventy-five million for the three years. See "The Demand for Cigarettes: Advertising the Health Scare and the Cigarette Advertising Ban," *Review of Economics and Statistics*, November 1972, p. 408. The FCC estimated fifty million for that period (in a personal letter from Marie Lawton of the American Cancer Society to Professor Dan Horsky of the Graduate School of Management, University of Rochester, June 23, 1975). The figure fifty million was also cited, in the January 1977 edition of *Madison Avenue* by Irving Rimer.

[39]See K. M. Friedman, *Public Policy and the Smoking-Health Controversy* (Lexington, Mass.: Lexington Books, 1975), p. 50.

[40]American Cancer Society, *op. cit.*, p. 51.

[41]Cited in K. M. Friedman, *op. cit.*, p. 51.

[42]See Appendix A.

[43]Public Law 91-222, April 1, 1970.

[44]Received in a private exchange by Dan Horsky of the Graduate School of Management of the University of Rochester from Helen Jones of the American Lung Association, August 7, 1975.

[45]See Kenneth J. Arrow, *The Limits of Organization* (New York: W. W. Norton, 1974), pp. 47-48.

Chapter Three

[1]In Chapter two we mentioned the problem created by the prohibition act and also noted that "drinking" was not covered under the Eighteenth Amendment. If it had been, many more Americans would have been considered to be performing illegal acts. See on this point also the discussion in William H. Riker and Peter C. Ordeshook, *An Introduction to Positive Political Theory* (New Jersey: Prentice-Hall, 1973), p. 289. See also their treatment of regulation and public policy, pp. 272-306.

[2]Note that society does not make decisions; people, as individuals, do. Arriving at an aggregate decision — "social," "public" outcome — usually involves a process which is political in essence.

[3]Robert C. North, "Conflict: Political Aspects" in David L. Sills (ed.), *International Encyclopedia of the Social Sciences* (New York: Free Press, 1968), vol. 3, p. 230.

[4]See Lewis R. Coser, "The Termination of Conflict" in the *Journal of Conflict Resolution* 5, no. 4, December 1961, p. 348.

[5]Setting up the ground rules for market activity is an important function that even the "minimalists" will not deny the government. See, for example, M. Friedman, *Capitalism and Freedom* (Chicago: University of Chicago Press, 1962), p. 34.

[6]Pendleton E. Herring, *Public Administration and the Public Interest* (New York: McGraw-Hill, 1936), p. 23.

[7]Although there is still a dispute in the economic and policy literature concerning the consequences of regulation in these and other fields, the evidence about the adverse outcomes of regulation when compared to their explicit goals is mounting. See, for example, Douglas M. Brown, *Introduction to Urban Economics* (New York: Academic Press, 1974) especially on housing regulation, pp. 128-164. B. H. Siegman, *Other Peoples' Property* (Lexington, Mass.: Lexington Books, 1976) on zoning. On the adverse results in the pharmaceutical industry see Sam Peltzman, *Regulation of Pharmaceutical Innovation: The 1962 Amendments* (Washington, D.C.: American Enterprise Institute for Public Policy Research, 1974). For a general summary of such adverisities, see Riker and Ordeshook, *op. cit.*, in particular, pp. 300-303.

[8]On the rationale to support the growers see Harold B. Rowe, *Tobacco under the AAA* (Washington, D.C.: Brookings Institution, 1935).

[9]See J. G. March and H. Simon, *Organizations* (New York: Wiley, 1958), p. 156.

[10]See Emmette S. Redford, "The Never Ending Search for the Public Interest," reprinted from E. S. Redford (ed.), *Ideals and Practices in Public Administration* (University, Ala.: University of Alabama Press, 1958), Bobbs-Merrill Reprint Series in the Social Sciences, PS-236, p. 136.

[11]See K. J. Arrow, *Social Choice and Individual Values*, 2nd ed. (New Haven: Yale University Press, 1963.

[12]On the nature of this competition see William N. Niskanen, Jr., *Bureaucracy and Representative Government* (Chicago: Aldine, 1971).

[13]See Richard M. Cyert and J. G. March, *A Behavioral Theory of the Firm* (New Jersey: Prentice-Hall, 1963), p. 27.

[14]See George J. Stigler, *The Citizen and the State* (Chicago: University of Chicago Press, 1975), p. 140.

[15]Charles E. Lindblom, *The Intelligence of Democracy* (New York: Free Press, 1965), p. 229.

[16]Stigler, *op. cit.*, p. 114.

[17]Co-optation is defined as "the process of absorbing new elements into the leadership or policy-determining structure of an organization as a means of averting threats to its stability or existence." See J. D. Thompson and W. J. McEwen, "Organizational Goals and Environment: Goal Setting as an Interaction Process," *American Sociological Review* 23, no. 1, February 1958, p. 27. For a classic study of cooptation see Philip Selznick, *TVA and the Grass Roots* (New York: Harper, 1966).

[18]See George Daly and David W. Brady, "Federal Regulation of Economic Activity: Failures and Reforms," in James E. Anderson (ed.), *Economic Regulatory Policies* (Lexington, Mass.: Lexington Books, 1976), p. 182. See also Fred A. Kramer, *Dynamics of Public Bureaucracy* (Cambridge, Mass.: Winthrop, 1977), Chap. 2.

[19]See Daly and Brady, *op. cit.*, p. 180.

[20]*Ibid.*

[21]Cyret and March, *op. cit.*, p. 27.

[22]See James Q. Wilson, "The Politics of Regulation," in James W. McKie (ed.), *Social Responsibility and the Business Predicament* (Washington, D.C.: Brookings Institution, 1974), pp. 155-168. See also Stigler, *op. cit.*

[23]See William H. Riker, *The Theory of Political Coalition* (New Haven: Yale University Press, 1962).

[24]On the assumption that firms are risk averse see Howard Raiffa, *Decision Analysis* (Reading, Mass.: Addison-Wesley, 1970), pp. 91-94.

[25]See Riker and Ordeshook, *op. cit.*, p. 191.

[26]See Arend Lijphart, "Consociational Democracy," in *World Politics* 21, no. 2, January 1969, pp. 207-227; Eric A. Nordlinger, *Conflict Regulation in Divided Societies* (Cambridge, Mass.: Center for International Affairs, Harvard University Press, 1972).

[27]Wilson, *op. cit.*, p. 141.

[28]Mancur Olson Jr., *The Logic of Collective Action* (Cambridge, Mass.: Harvard University Press, 1965), pp. 48-50.

[29]The concept of "externalities" used in this study is broad and close to the political definition that was given by John Dewey in *The Public and Its Problems* (New York: Henry Holt, 1927), pp. 15-16. It is not used in the strict economic sense. See Richard A. Musgrave and Peggy B. Musgrave, *Public Finance in Theory and Practice* (New York: McGraw-Hill, 1973).

[30]Although it is assumed that the firm is a profit maximizer, some economic scholars propose that the firm is rather a revenue (sales) maximizer. See, for example, William J. Baumol, "The Revenue Maximization Hypothesis," in M. L. Joseph, N. C. Seeber and C. L. Bach (eds.), *Economic Analysis and Policy* (New Jersey: Prentice-Hall, 1963) pp. 220-226. Although we recognize that there may be "some conflict between the firm's sales goals and its profit objectives" (p. 225), we nevertheless, for reasons of simplification, treat both goals interchangeably.

[31]The assumption of profit maximization as a firm's goal is not restricted, of course, to the short run. It sometimes seems as if firms are engaged or invest in activities that have nothing to do with their economic goals, such as philanthropy, development of the environment, and so on. Such activities are not deduced from some notion of responsibility of the firm to society but rather should be understood as a practical matter — an investment in public relations where returns will be collected in the long run. On this issue see Henry G. Manne and Henry C. Wallich, *The Modern Corporation and Social Responsibility* (Washington, D.C.: American Enterprise Institute for Public Policy Research, 1972).

[32]See Stigler, *op. cit.*, p. 31.

[33]There are other sources of uncertainty which the industry has to deal with, for example, technological changes that help the rival firms improve quality cost, marketing actions taken by competitors, and so on. On this and on the way a firm approaches the uncertainty problem see Francesco M. Nicosia, "Industry Point of View on Advertising: Some Problems Searching for Answers," in S. F. Divita (ed.), *Advertising and the Public Interest* (Chicago: American Marketing Association, 1974), pp. 45-55.

[34]A. Cournot, *Researches into the Mathematical Principles of the Theory of Wealth* (New York: Macmillan, 1897).

[35]Jesse W. Markham, "Oligopoly," in Sills, *op. cit.*, p. 284.

[36]For example, E. H. Chamberlin, *The Theory of Monopolistic Competition*, (Cambridge, Mass.: Harvard Economic Studies, 1956, 7th ed.) R. M. Cyret and J. G. March, "Organizational Structure and Pricing Behavior in Oligopolistic Market," *American Economic Review* 45, 1955, pp. 129-139; J. W. Markham, "The Nature and Significance of Price Leadership," *American Economic Review* 41, 1951, pp. 891-905; W. J. Fellner, *Competition among Few* (New York: Knopf, 1949); J. Von Neumann and O. Morgenstern, *Theory of Games and Economic Behavior* (New York: John Wiley, 1944); M. Shubik, *Strategy and Market Structure* (New York: John Wiley, 1959); James W. Friedman, *Oligopoly and the Theory of Games* (New York: North-Holland Pub. Co., 1977); M. Nicholson, *Oligopoly and Conflict* (Toronto: University of Toronto, 1972); Robert Sherman, *Oligopoly: An Empirical Approach* (Lexington, Mass.: Lexington Books, 1972).

[37]See Markham, in Sills, *op. cit.*, p. 289.

[38]See references 19 and 22 to Chapter two.

[39]The disincentive to compete by price due to the high portion of the fixed cost was pointed out by Nicholls in *Price Policies in the Cigarette Industry* (Nashville: Vanderbilt University Press, 1951). The gross marginal profit

appears in Dan Horsky, "Optimal Advertising Strategy under Dynamic Market Conditions" (Lafayette, Ind.: Kranmert Graduate School of Industrial Administration, Purdue University, Ph.D. dissertation, 1974), p. 83. Similarly in Frank M. Bass "A Simulation Equation Regression Study of Advertising and Sales of Cigarettes," *Journal of Marketing Research* VI, August 1969, p. 296.

[40] J. K. Galbraith, *The New Industrial State* (Boston: Houghton Mifflin, 1967), pp. 198-210.

[41] See Robert M. Solow, "The Truth Further Refined: A Comment on Morris," *The Public Interest,* no. 11, Spring 1968, p. 48.

[42] Raymond A Bauer and Stephen A. Greyser, *Advertising in America: The Consumer View* (Boston: Harvard Graduate School of Business Administration, 1970), p. 90.

[43] See James M. Ferguson, "Comment," in *Journal of Law and Economics* 19, August 1976, pp. 341-342. See also Ferguson's *Advertising and Competition: Theory, Measurement, Fact* (Cambridge, Mass.: Ballinger, 1974) and Philip Nelson, "The Economic Value of Advertising," in Y. Brozen (ed.), *Advertising and Society* (New York: New York University Press, 1974), pp. 44-62.

[44] Nelson, *op. cit.,* p. 52. The experience goods may be further divided into durable and non-durable goods. The latter (e.g., cosmetics) are usually advertised more.

[45] See Baumol, *op. cit.,* Cyret and March, *op. cit.,* and Horsky, *op. cit.,* for an explanation of the market share argument.

[46] For reasons of theoretical parsimony we ignore other marketing activities such as better service, nicer packaging, and so on. Since they may be interpreted as "information," we include them under the single umbrella of advertising strategy.

[47] That the advertising of one firm may cancel the effect of the advertising of another firm was recognized by Robert Dorfman in *The Price System* (Englewood Cliffs, N. J.: Prentice-Hall, 1964), p. 102.

[48] Shubik, *op. cit.,* pp. 318-319.

[49] *Ibid.,* p. 320, specifies these strategies.

[50] See Stigler, *op. cit.,* p. 116. Note that in the case of the cigarette industry, subsidies are given directly to the tobacco grower.

[51] This was more or less the response of the cigarette industry. See K. M. Friedman, *Public Policy and the Smoking-Health Controversy* (Lexington,

Mass.: Lexington Books, 1975), p. 22.

[52]Competition in oligopoly as a prisoners' dilemma game was dealt with by several economists. See for example Sherman, *op. cit.* Although Sherman deals primarily with the price of the product and its capacity limit, he is also aware that " . . . moreover . . . firms might compete by advertising rather than price. Doing so could limit the amount of their excess profit, though, so high advertising need not be associated with high profit" (p. 179). Since we cannot specify the payoff structure in our demonstration, we say that this situation *resembles* the prisoners' dilemma. Thus only the logic is employed, On such games see Anatol Rappoport and Albert M. Chammah, *Prisoners' Dilemma* (Ann Arbor: University of Michigan Press, 1965).

[53]A study of 984 top political executives conducted in 1965 showed that fifty-five percent went on to business or other professions. Out of these, twenty-one percent returned to the organization they originally came from, three percent returned to previous businesses that were related to federal executive work, five percent to unrelated fields, and three percent entered new businesses related to federal executive work. See David T. Stanley, Deon E. Mann and Jameson W. Doig, *Men Who Govern* (Washington, D.C.: Brookings Institution, 1967), p. 161.

[54]Apart from E. Drew's description, such was the case in the 1965 Label Case. See "The Quiet Victory of the Cigarette Lobby." A recent example demonstrated the intention of the cigarette industry to shift the battle from the Civil Aeronautics Board (C.A.B.), who wished to regulate the percentage of seats guaranteed to smokers and non-smokers, to the Congress, where the industry expects a favorable regulation. See "Eastern Airlines Agrees to Ban Smoking in Sixty-Five Percent of Plane Seats," *New York Times* June 15, 1977, pp. 1 and 15.

[55]Thomas C. Schelling, *The Strategy of Conflict* (Cambridge, Mass.: Harvard University Press, 1960).

[56]On the diffusion process see Robert Eyestone, "Confusion, Diffusion. and Innovation," *American Political Science Review* 71, June 1977, pp. 441-447.

[57]Nelson, *op. cit.*, p. 54.

[58]Brozen, *op. cit.*, p. 84.

[59]Lester Telser, *Advertising and Competition* (London: Institute of Economic Affairs, occasional paper 4, 1965), p. 31.

[60]*Ibid.*, p. 29.

Chapter Four

[1] See *Congressional Quarterly Almanac* 1965, p. 349.

[2] See *Congressional Weekly Report* nos. 13, 26, 1965, p. 534.

[3] *Ibid.*

[4] See, for example, Cuyler E. Jammond et al., *Some Recent Findings Concerning Cigarette Smoking,* presented at a meeting on "The Origins of Human Cancer" at Cold Spring Harbor Laboratory on September 14, 1976.

[5] Reduction of the level of cigarette consumption is also the explicit goal of the American Cancer Society; see *Task Force on Tobacco and Health, Target 5,*1976, p. 13.

[6] When price of products and personal disposable income are included in a consumption model they tend to generate the statistical pathology known as "multicollinearity." This is because both factors tend to rise simultaneously over time. A model that contains collinear variables may have good predictive power. Also, there are some suggested techniques for bypassing this problem. On the problem of multicollinearity and what to do about it, see John H. Aldrich, *A Two Step Procedure for Analysis in the Presence of Multicollinearity,* paper delivered at the April 1977 meeting of the Midwest Political Science Association, Chicago. A different technique, i.e., the interaction variable procedure, was suggested by J. A. Senquist in *Multivariate Model Building* (Ann Arbor, Mich.: ISR, 1970), pp. 1-25.

[7] Such variable construction, considering the two factors simultaneously, not only bypasses the problem mentioned in note 6 but is also higher in information content and therefore an improvement from a policy point of view. It must be assumed, however, that the demand for cigarettes is not perfectly inelastic.

[8] See U.S. Department of Commerce, Bureau of the Census, *Statistical Abstract of the United States* (Washington, D.C.: U.S. Government Printing Office, 1976), no. 641, p. 400; 1975, no. 622, p. 386; 1970, no. 480, p. 316; 1965, no. 455, p. 331; 1958, no. 389, p. 308; 1956, no. 357, p. 297. Prices were converted to 1952 base. This publication compiles information from many sources. The original source for disposable income was U.S. Bureau of Economic Analysis, Survey of Current Business.

[9] See Tobacco Tax Council, *The Tax Burden on Tobacco,* vol. 11, Richmond, Virginia, 1976.

[10] See David Shapiro et al. "Smoking on Cue: A Behavioral Approach to Smoking Reduction," *Journal of Health and Social Behavior* 12, June 1971, p. 109. See also Caroline S. Keutzer et al. "Modification of Smoking Be-

havior: A Review," *Psychological Bulletin* 70, December 1968, pp. 520-533.

[11]On the rationale for lagging "once and for all" see R. Rao and R. I. Miller, *Applied Econometrics* (California: Wodsworth, 1971), pp. 161-173. Similarly, on "koyck lag" see also J. Johnston, *Econometric Methods* (New York: McGraw-Hill, 1972), pp. 292-302.

[12]By utilizing the lagged variable as we did, we substantially simplified the model. Simple models, according to Carl Hempel, are to be prized highly "because they tell us more, because their empirical content is greater and because they are better tested." See C. G. Hempel, *Philosophy of Natural Science* (Englewood Cliffs, N. J.: Prentice-Hall, 1976), p. 44.

[13]Several scholars have utilized percapitization procedures in their studies on cigarette consumption. See, for example, Robert K. Miller, *Tobacco and Tobacco Products Consumption for 1985* (Washington, D.C.: United States Department of Agriculture, Economic Research Service, 1973).

[14]For example, see F. M. Bass, "A Simulation Equation Regresson Study of Advertising and Sales of Cigarettes," *Journal of Marketing Research* 6, August 1969; J. C. Hamilton, "The Demand for Cigarettes," *Review of Economics and Statistics*, November 1972; Miller, *op. cit.*, and E. R. Tufte, *Data Analysis for Politics and Policy* (Englewood Cliffs, N. J.: Prentice-Hall, 1974), p. 82.

[15]Yankelovich, Skelly and White, *Teenage Boys and Girls and Cigarette Smoking* (New York: American Cancer Society, February, 1976).

[16]Data on the various age groups were compiled from the Bureau of the Census in the Department of Commerce; for the period 1970-1975, we used *Population Estimates and Projection,* series P-25, no. 614, December 1975 pp. 17-22; for 1960-1970, *Population Estimates and Projections*, P-25, no. 483, April 1970, p. 3; for 1954-1959, *Estimates of Population of the U.S.: By Single Year, by Age, Color and Sex: 1900-1959,* July 2, 1965.

[17]See *Advertising Age*, "Costs of Cigarette Advertising: 1975-1968," November 22, 1976, pp. 36-38; "Costs of Cigarette Advertising: 1969-1961," October 12, 1970, pp. 19-20; "Costs of Cigarette Advertising: 1965-1957," July 25, 1966, pp. 56-58; "Costs of Cigarette Advertising: 1959-1952," September 19, 1960. The only brand not ranked by *Advertising Age* but included in the sample is Reynolds' 1975 More.

[18]See Appendix B. As a matter of fact, information covering 1953 was also compiled, the reason being that we had anticipated a loss of at least one observation which usually occurs when correction for autocorrolation is undertaken. Since the model includes a lagged dependent variable as an independent one, we felt that such a correction was unavoidable.

[19] See Harry M. Wootten, in *Printer's Ink* December 30, 1955, p. 13; December 28, 1956, p. 29; December 27, 1957, p. 23; December 26, 1958, p. 23; December 25, 1959, pp. 20-21; December 27, 1960; December 22, 1961, p. 25; John C. Maxwell, Jr., replaced Wootten and published "The Maxwell Report" in the same publication in February 14, 1964; December 18, 1964; December 10, 1965; December 9, 1966. In 1967 it appeared in *Marketing/Communications,* November 1967, and in 1968 in *Tobacco Reporter,* November 1968, December 1970, November 1971, November 1972, November 1973, April 1975, November 1976. I would like to thank the Tobacco Merchants Association of the United States for providing this information.

[20] See, for example, T. McGuiness and K. Cowling, "Advertising and the Aggregate Demand for Cigarettes," *European Economic Review* 6, no. 3, July 1975.

[21] R. Schmalensee, in attempting to construct a "message" measurement, employed several strong assumptions, in addition to extrapolation and interpolation methods, to cover missing data. See, for example, the description in the three appendixes to his book, *The Economics of Advertising* (Amsterdam: North Holland, 1972), pp. 245-275.

[22] The information about advertising was compiled from *National Advertising Investments (LNA),* vols. 5-25 (1954-1973). Figures for the years 1974 and 1975 were compiled from *Ad $ Summary (LNA).*

[23] *Advertising Age* fully covers the television and radio expenditures. *LNA* covered only network expenditures and spot television for a few years only. Since identical coverage was given by both publications to the printed media, subtraction of *LNA's* print figures from *Advertising Age's* total figures generated the broadcasting variable.

[24] "Consumer Price Index" appears in *Statistical Abstract of the United States,* under "purchasing power of the dollar," 1976, no. 699, p. 432. The base year (1967) was converted by setting 1952 = 100 and calculating accordingly.

[25] Local taxes also add to the price of the product, but since it is very difficult, if not impossible, to acquire information on them, we will not consider them in the analysis to follow.

[26] Vol. 11, 1976.

[27] Figures for state populations were taken from *Statistical Abstract of the United States* 1976, table no. 10, p. 11; 1975, no. 11, p. 12; 1973, no. 13, p. 13; 1968, no. 11, p. 12; 1967, no. 10, p. 12; and 1958 Table no. 6, p.10.

[28]See Edward R. Tufte, "Improving Data Analysis in Political Science," in
E. R. Tufte (ed.), *The Quantitative Analysis of Social Science* (Reading,
Mass.: Addison-Wesley, 1970), p. 439.

[29]The only two states that did not behave according to this pattern were Utah
(low tax, low consumption) and Nevada (high tax, high consumption). This
is clearly accounted for if we remember that the Mormon religious code is
unsympathetic to smoking (Utah) and that the tourist industry and the
free cigarettes given by the casinos raise the level in Nevada.

[30]On the theoretical expectation of autocorrelation due to the presence of
lagged dependent variables in the model and the consequences to the
parameter estimators and their interpretation, see D. A. Hibbs, Jr., "Problems of Statistical Estimation and Causal Inferences in Time Series Regression Models," in L. H. Costner (ed.), *Sociological Methodology, 1973-
1974* (San Francisco: Jossey Bass, 1974). The Durbin-Watson test for
detecting autocorrelation in ordinary least squares regression may not provide meaningful information and may not be appropriate if one of the
independent variables consists of lagged values of the dependent variable.
See J. Thomas, *Notes on the Theory of Multiple Regression Analysis*
(Athens, Ga.: Center of Economic Research, 1964), p. 111.

[31]On this technique see Hibbs, *op. cit.*, pp. 249-299; also his *Mass Political Vio-
lence* (New York: John Wiley, 1973), pp. 135-231; and H. H. Kelejian
and W. E. Oates, *Introduction to Econometrics* (New York: Harper and
Row, 1974), pp. 176-206. There are computer programs geared to correct
the autocorrelation problem utilizing this technique. One such program
is Troll, maintained by the National Bureau of Economic Research. I
would like to thank Professor Peter Lemieux from the University of Rochester for assisting me in the utilization of this program.

[32]The following discussion is based on the idea advanced by A. S. Goldberger;
see his *Impact Multipliers and Dynamic Properties* (Amsterdam: North-
Holland, 1959). See also A. S. Goldberger, "The Economist's Role in
Policy Formation," in P. A. Yotopoulos (ed.), *Economic Analysis and
Economic Policy* (Athens, Ga.: Center of Planning and Economic Research,
1966), pp. 17-22; G. Fromm and P. Taubman, *Policy Simulation With
Econometric Model* (Washington, D.C.: Brookings Institution, 1968);
and D. A. Hibbs, Jr., "On Analyzing the Effects of Policy Intervention:
Box-Jenkins and Box-Tiao vs. Structural Equation Models," in D. R. Heise
(ed.), *Sociological Methodology, 1977* (San Francisco: Jossey-Bass, 1977),
pp. 137-179.

[33]See M. Ray and W. Wilke, "Fear: The Potential of an Appeal Neglected by
Marketing," *Journal of Marketing*, January 1970, pp. 54-62.

[34]That this objective is unrealistic is suggested by the high value of the constant term (*a*). This value constitutes almost thirty percent of the average per capita sales for model (2.2). Although it is very difficult to translate the meaning of the entry (intercept) in econometric interpretation of mathematical models (as distinguished from straightforward mathematical models) we nevertheless suggest, in a very rough sense, that the intercept touches the "primary demand" for the product. That is, regardless of the effects of other independent variables, there does exist some level of "need" in the population for the product. On the problems involved in the interpretation of the constant term see, Rao and Miller, *op. cit.*, p. 5.

[35]That a policy maker is a "satisficer" rather than maximizer was suggested by Herbert Simon; see his book *Models of Man* (New York: John Wiley, 1957), and also his work with J. G. March, *Organizations* (New York: John Wiley, 1958).

[36]That policies and decisions are made in an attempt to affect the margin of a given phenomenon was proposed by Charles Lindblom; see his article "The Science of Muddling Through," *Public Administration Review* 19, 1959, pp. 79-88. See also his book with David Braybrook, *A Strategy of Decision* (New York: Free Press, 1970).

[37]See, for example, "Cut in Cigarette Tax is Backed in Albany," *New York Times*, March 13, 1977, p. 44. The gross profit of organized crime from cigarette bootlegging is estimated by *Time* to be 1.5 billion dollars — see May 16, 1977, p. 36.

[38]See L. E. Wynder and D. Hoffman, *Tobacco and Tobacco Smoke* (New York: Academic Press, 1967), p. 114. See also citations in Tufte, "Data Analysis," *loc. cit.*, p. 83.

[39]Julian L. Simon, *Issues in the Economics of Advertising* (Chicago: University of Illinois Press, 1970), p. 252.

[40]See Horsky, "Optional Advertising Strategy under Dynamic Market Conditions," Kramment Graduate School of Industrial Administration, Purdue University, Ph.D. dissertation, 1974, p. 1.

[41]Cited in Hamilton, "The Demand for Cigarettes," *loc. cit.*, p. 401.

[42]*Ibid.*, pp. 110-111.

[43]See Dan Horsky, "Market Share Response to Advertising: An Example of Theory Testing," *Journal of Marketing Research* 24, February 1977, pp. 17-18.

[44]See Yoram Peles, "Rates of Amortization of Advertising Expenditures," *Journal of Political Economy* 74, September-October 1971, pp. 1032-1059.

[45] For example, between 1967 and 1970, American's Carlton cost thirty-five cents on the average. Virginia Slim (Philip Morris) cost an average of twenty-four cents; Lorillard's True, twenty-eight cents; Lark (Liggett and Myers) twenty-three, and so on.

[46] See Edmund Faltermayer, "Reynolds Gets a Bang out of the Cigarette Brand Explosion," *Fortune*, October 1976, p. 138.

[47] *Ibid.*, p. 226.

[48] *Ibid.*, p. 138

[49] Ann Crittenden, "40 Million for a Real Smoke," *New York Times*, May 15, 1977, pp. 4-5.

[50] Philip Dougherty, "New Low Tar, High Budget Smoke," *New York Times*, June 20, 1977, p. 44.

[51] See *News and Observer*, October 31, 1971.

Chapter Five

[1] See James Wilson, in J. W. McKie (ed.), *Social Responsibility and the Business Predicament* (Washington, D.C.: Brookings Institution, 1974), p. 139. The theory of self-interest was categorized by Stigler in the following colorful way: "The second view of the regulation of industry is essentially an imponderable, unpredictive mixture of forces of the most diverse nature, comprehending acts of great moral virtue and the most vulgar venality" (the congressman feathering his own nest). See G. J. Stigler, *The Citizen and the State* (Chicago: University of Chicago Press, 1975), p. 114. For a debate expressed from the two viewpoints, see M. E. Cohen and G. J. Stigler, *Can Regulatory Agencies Protect Consumers?* (Washington, D.C.: American Enterprise Institute for Public Policy Research, 1971).

[2] This list was taken from K. Friedman, *Public Policy and the Smoking-Health Controversy* (Lexington, Mass.: Lexington Books, 1975), p. 191.

[3] A.L. Fritschler, *Smoking and Politics: Policy Making and the Federal Bureaucracy* (New York: Meredith Corporation, 1969), p. 3.

[4] On congressmen as maximizers of their probability to be re-elected, see David R. Mayhew, *Congress: the Electoral Connection* (New Haven: Yale University Press, 1974).

[5] These two million dollars were approved by the Congress in 1965 in order to establish a national clearinghouse on smoking and health in the Public Health Service (PHS). See *Congressional Quarterly Almanac* 1969, p. 883.

120   *References*

Later on, subsidies were given by the FCC to the health coalition under the Fairness Doctrine.

[6]On the size of groups and its effect on the ability to act collectively, see Mancur Olson, Jr., *The Logic of Collective Action* (Cambridge, Mass.: Harvard University Press, 1965), p. 36.

[7]On the size of the coalition and the sharing of payoffs among its members, see William Riker, *The Theory of Political Coalitions* (New Haven: Yale University Press, 1962).

[8]Friedman, *op. cit.* p. 161.

[9]Wilson, *op. cit.*, p. 141-142.

[10]This remark is attributed to Herbert Legget who wrote it as a commentary for the Valley National Bank of Phoenix, Arizona. See John Larson (ed.), *The Regulated Businessman* (New York: Holt, Rinehart and Winston, 1966), p. 206.

[11]Smith, Barney and Co., *The Cigarette Industry*, Topical Research Comment, no. 97-69, N.Y., December 1968, pp. 1-2.

[12]The information about ranking was taken from "Who Did Best (and Worst) Among the 500," *The Fortune Directory of Ten 500 Largest Industrial Corporations* (New York: Time Corporation, August 1965), pp. 20-23; October 1966, pp. 22-25; May 1969, pp. 24-27. Brown and Williamson, being a British subsidiary, is not included. Also, non-cigarette tobacco companies are included, for example, Universal Leaf Tobacco of Richmond, Virginia. The information on the position of the cigarette companies after the 1960s is less reliable, due to the fact that all had diversified and taken other lines of products and most had changed their names. Thus the American Tobacco Company is today called American Brands; Brown and Wiliamson is British American Tobacco Company; Lorillard joined the Loews Corporation.

[13]This upward trend which started in 1970 and continued throughout 1971 reversed itself in the following years. In 1975, the industry showed the best performance as far as increased sales and profits among the twenty-eight industries ranked by *Fortune*. See the *Fortune Directory*, 1971, 1972, pp. 24-27; *Fortune 500*, May 1976, pp. 338-341. These figures, however, are less reliable. See note 12.

[14]John C. Maxwell, Jr., "The 1976 Maxwell Report on Cigarettes," *Tobacco Reporter*, November 16, 1976, p. 54.

[15]R. J. Reynolds, in its low-tar-and-nicotine process "puffs" the tobacco; American dries the tobacco in order to prevent it from shrinking. Other

firms use similar processes. The idea is to get more air and less tobacco in the same dimension of cigarette. On the process and the saving, see *Advertising Age*, December 1, 1969, p. 78.

[16] Reports on these findings are given by Walter S. Rose, "Poison Gas in Your Cigarettes," *Reader's Digest*, December 1976, pp. 92-98.

[17] See "The Chemistry of Smoking," *Time*, February 21, 1977, p. 48.

[18] See *CQA* 1969, p. 888.

[19] That advertising inhibits market competition and its elimination restricts the scope of such competition was discussed by Lester Telser in *Advertising and Competition* (London: Institute of Economic Affairs, 1965). See also additional references in Chapter three.

[20] *Advertising Age*, September 13, 1976, p. 120.

[21] See "Little Cigar Broadcasting Ban" in *CQA* 1973, p. 403.

[22] *Tobacco*, March 17, 1972.

[23] See Nicholas von Hoffman in *New York Post*, October 30, 1975.

[24] *Ibid.*

[25] *United States Tobacco Journal*, November 11, 1976, p. 11. See also *ibid.*, October 12, 1976, pp. 3 and 18.

[26] They will allow, however, the advertisement of low-tar-and-nicotine cigarettes. See American Cancer Society *Task Force on Smoking and Health*, *Target 5*, 1976, p. 29.

[27] *Ibid.*, p. 8.

[28] *Ibid.*

[29] See Irving Rimer, "American Cancer Society: Antismoking Advertising Works," *Madison Avenue*, January 1977.

[30] See "House and Senate Disagree on Cigarette Ad Bill," *CQA* 1969, p. 887.

[31] As cited by Marvin E. Goldberg and Gerald J. Gorn, "An Experimental Approach to the Effect of Television Advertising on Children," in S. F. Divita (ed.), *Advertising and the Public Interest* (Chicago: American Marketing Association, 1974), p. 149.

[32] These remarks were made by Fred Decker, publisher of *Printers' Ink*. See John C. Maxwell, Jr., "Winstons Press Pall Malls for the Lead," *Printers' Ink*, December 10, 1965, p. 16.

[33] See "Maxwell Report," *Printers' Ink,* December 18, 1964, p. 26.

[34] See *Business Week,* November 21, 1970. This information was released by George Weisman, President of Philip Morris. *Business Week* was among the first to suggest a ban on television and radio cigarette commercials, as far back as 1959. See "Clearing Smoke from the Airwaves," April 5, 1959, pp. 38-39. It also predicted a continued drop in sales of cigarettes after 1970, which was of course wrong; see "A Friendly Rivalry Goes Up in Smoke," June 20, 1970.

[35] The following discussion is based primarily on the various publications of *Congressional Quarterly Almanac;* see "Smoking Linked to Disease: Government Action Delayed," vol. XX, 1964, pp. 246-252; "Health Warning Required on Cigarette Packs," vol. XXI, 1965, pp. 344-351; "Smoking Reports," vol. XXIV, 1968, p. 707; "House and Senate Disagree on Cigarette Advertising Bill," vol. XXV, 1969, pp. 883-890; "Ban on Cigarette Radio and Television Advertising Enacted," vol. XXVI, 1970, pp. 145-146. Unless otherwise indicated, all citations are taken from these sources.

[36] See Gary Lessner and John C. Maxwell, Jr., "Ad Man's Inside Track to Money — A Sequel," *Marketing/Communications,* November 1967, p. 34. As a matter of fact, Maxwell predicted in 1965 that if consumption was not reduced because of the labelling requirement, the antismoking forces will "press for more remedial action," i.e., further regulation of advertising. See John Maxwell, Jr., in *Printers' Ink,* December 10, 1965, p. 16.

[37] See *CQA* 1971, p. 497.

[38] At least as far as the data go, and probably for the next five to ten years. For the statement of the goal see *CQA* 1965, p. 349. See also for discussion in Chapter four.

[39] For representative examples of such literature see Peter O. Steiner, "The Public Sector and the Public Interest," in R. H. Haveman and J. Margolis (eds.), *Public Expenditures and Policy Analysis* (Chicago: Markham, 1970), pp. 21-58. See also R. A. Musgrave and P. B. Musgrave, *Public Finance in Theory and Practice* (New York: McGraw-Hill, 1973) and J. G. Head, "Public Goods and Public Policy" in *Public Finance,* no. 3, 1962, pp. 197-221.

[40] In the market place the only "coercive" force is the price system. On the differences between the political and economic market and the role of government, see F. A. Hayek, *Economic Freedom and Representative Government* (London: Institute of Economic Affairs, 1973).

[41] But see R. Coase, "The Problem of Social Cost," *Journal of Law and Economics* 3, October 1960, pp. 1-44.

[42] See R. Posner, *Regulation of Advertising by the FTC* (Washington, D.C.: American Enterprise Institute for Public Policy Research, Evaluative Studies, November 11, 1973), p. 7.

[43] See "Controversial Cigarette Tax Proposal Aired," in *CQ Weekly Report*, April 10, 1976, pp. 844-848.

[44] See John C. Maxwell, Jr., "The 1976 Maxwell Report on Cigarettes," *Tobacco Reporter*, November 1976, p. 54.

[45] See D. F. Mullally, "The Fairness Doctrine: Benefits and Cost," *Public Opinion Quarterly* 33, Winter 1969-1970, p. 578.

[46] See T. O'Keefe, "The Anti-Smoking Commercials: A Study of Television Impact on Behavior," *Public Opinion Quarterly* 35, Summer 1971, p. 147. O'Keefe reports that only ten percent of the 921 people sampled in his study had never seen a single antismoking commercial, although eighty to one hundred commercials were aired each week.

[47] *Ibid.*, p. 148.

[48] 8 FCC 2nd 381, FCC 2nd 921.

[49] See Lee Loevinger, "The Politics of Advertising," in Divita (ed.), *op. cit.*, p. 2.

[50] *Retail Store Employees* v. *FCC*, 463 F2d 248, D.C. cir. 1970; and *Friends of the Earth* v. *FCC*, 449 F2d 1164, D.C. cir. 1971.

[51] Loevinger, *op. cit.*, argues forcefully against the Fairness Doctrine and the FTC proposals of counter-advertising. He thinks that counter-advertising, among other things, will (a) destroy the economic foundation of the broadcasting industry; (b) make broadcasting a far less attractive advertising media; (c) not be informative; (d) increase government power and its control over the market; and (e) be unfair to honest advertising.

[52] *Larus and Brother Company et al.* v. *FCC*, U.S. Court of Appeals, no. 15, 382, 1971, pp. 10 and 17.

[53] *CQA* 1970, p. 146.

[54] See Jerome Rothenberg, "The Physical Environment," in McKie (ed.), *op. cit.*, p. 207.

[55] See C. W. Churchman, *Prediction and Optimal Decision* (Englewood Cliffs, N.J.: Prentice-Hall, 1961).

[56] See "Tobacco Road: Smuggling Smoke is Not a Victimless Crime," *Time* November 14, 1977, p. 84.

Appendix A

Chronology of Federal Commissions' Interventions
in the Market Practices of the Cigarette Industry

(Sources: See text, Fritschler, the Tobacco Institute, *New York Times, Advertising Age*)

1955

September 15:   FTC promulgates cigarette advertising guides, prohibiting health claims, direct or indirect.

1959

December 17:   FTC writes to all cigarette firms that "all representation of low or reduced tar or nicotine, whether by filtration or otherwise, will be construed as health claims."

1960

January 14:   FTC tells cigarette manufacturers to omit from cigarette advertising reference, direct or implied, to health benefits to be derived from filter and reduced tar cigarettes.

1964

January 18:   A week after the release of the *Surgeon General's Report,* the FTC announces initiation of rulemaking proceedings pertaining to the advertising and labelling of cigarettes.

June 22:   FTC rules that all cigarette advertising and packaging will carry the following warning: "Cigarette smoking is *dangerous* to health and may cause *death* from cancer and other diseases." The requirement should take effect January 1, 1965 (advertising), July 1, 1965 (packaging).

1965

July 28:   FTC enacts trade rule "in keeping with congressional directive."

1966

March 25:   FTC reverses its 1955 and 1957 requirement and notifies the industry that it will no longer consider "a factual statement of tar and nicotine content" to be a health claim.

April 11:   The change in the position is explained. The FTC could no longer find expert witnesses to help sustain the charge that such disclosure would be misleading to the public.

June 8:   FTC reports to Senator Magnuson that it will establish a laboratory to test the tar and nicotine content of major cigarette brands in the market.

1967

January 5:   John F. Banzhaf III files a Fairness Doctrine complaint with the FCC against WCBS-TV. The FCC rules that the Fairness Doctrine applies to cigarette advertising.

June 5:   FCC rules that stations which broadcast cigarette commercials *must* also air antismoking commercials under the Fairness Doctrine.

June 30:   FTC recommends to Congress that "a statement setting forth the tar and nicotine content of each cigarette should be required to appear on the package and in all cigarette advertising."

November 22:   FTC publishes results of the first semi-annual test on tar and nicotine content in cigarettes.

December 5:   In a letter to the NAB, FCC commissioner Cox writes that stations which refuse cigarette spots but carry antismoking messages must give time to tobacco spokesmen, but the time does not have to be free.

1968

June 12:   Banzhaf's ASH files with the FCC the first of many petitions seeking revocation of station licenses for failure to provide sufficient time to antismoking commercials.

July 30:   FTC again recommends legislation for a mandatory health warning in advertising.

November 21:   U.S. Court of Appeals upholds the FCC application of Fairness Doctrine.

1969

February 5:   FCC issues notice of proposed rule-making to ban broadcast of cigarette advertising in the absence of voluntary action by the cigarette manufacturers.

April 17:   Testifying before the House Commerce Committee on cigarette labelling and advertising, FCC chairman Hyde says, "if we ban advertising . . . I would hope that the presentation on each side of the issue would be comparable . . . they [the stations, that would carry antismoking messages] would be subject, under the Fairness Doctrine, to the duty of making some reasonable provision for the presentation of the other side of the argument."

May 20:   FTC announces proposed rule-making procedure for requiring a more forceful health warning on cigarette packages.

July 1-2:   FTC has a hearing on the proposed rule to require that all cigarette advertising contain the warning that "Cigarette smoking is dangerous to health and may cause death from cancer, coronary heart disease, chronic bronchitis, pulmonary emphysema and other diseases."

July 22:   FTC chairman Dixon, in a written statement for the Senate Commerce Committee, says that the "commission would be disposed to suspend its now pending trade regulation rule proceeding until 1971, if cigarettes go off the air voluntarily or by legislative action." FCC chairman Hyde, when asked by Senator Moss if voluntary withdrawal would make appropriate "the continuance of those so-called anti or educational broadcasts" says, "I think it would be very appropriate . . . and the issue will continue to be a controversial one of public importance."

1970

August 8:   FTC proposes a rule requiring tar and nicotine listing in all cigarette advertising.

December 15: FCC rules that as of January 2, 1971, the Fairness Doctrine will cease to apply to smoking.

December 17: FTC accepts industry proposal to voluntarily display FTC tar-nicotine scores in all its advertisements.

1971

February 26: FTC recommends in an annual report to Congress the following legislation: stronger, front panel health warning on cigarette packages, larger appropriations for anticigarette commercials, "tar and nicotine disclosure on packs, appropriations for research toward developing a cigarette not hazardous to health."

June 11:   FCC initiates "a broad-ranging inquiry into the efficacy of the Fairness Doctrine and other commission public interest policies in the light of current demands for access to the broadcasting media to consider issues of public concern."

July 1:   FTC rules not to activate its congressionally embargoed pro-
                posal to require a severe health warning in cigarette ads.
                Instead, they will negotiate with each firm to require the
                package warning to show in cigarette ads in a more clear
                and conspicuous manner.

1972

January 24:   FTC annual report to Congress includes no legislative recom-
                mendation.

1973

January 24:   FTC turns down a petition from Banzhaf, requesting that the
                commission move immediately to ban broadcast ads of little
                cigars, saying any action should be handled by Congress.

May: CAB (Civil Aeronautics Board) orders commercial airliners
                to separate smokers from non-smokers.

September: CPSC (Consumer Product Safety Commission) chairman
                Simpson publishes the commission's "consumer product
                hazard index" which puts tobacco in an area of "question-
                able jurisdiction."

1974

February 6:   Banzhaf petitions the FTC to ban cigarette billboard advertis-
                ing.

April 1:   ICC (Interstate Commerce Commission) rules to limit twenty
                percent of seating space on interstate buses to smoking passen-
                gers.

April: FTC begins investigation of the size of the warning required
                in cigarette advertising.

July 2:   FCC limits the application of Fairness Doctrine only to broad-
                cast viewpoints rather than product commercials.

August 13:   FTC reports the biggest annual increase in cigarette sales
                since 1963 and a decrease in advertising expenditures.

September: CPSC rejects a furniture manufacturer's petition to regulate
                cigarette burning time.

1975

October 25:   FTC takes fifty thousand dollars from the National Institute
                of Health to set up tests of carbon monoxide yields in ciga-
                rettes.

1976

May: Ralph Nader asks the FAA (Federal Aviation Agency) to pro-
                     hibit smoking in airplane cockpits. President Ford signs
                     legislation to exempt tobacco from CPSC regulation. ICC
                     issues an order to prohibit smoking in railroad dining cars
                     and to require separate passenger cars for smokers and non-
                     smokers.

July 28:   FTC attorney Richard Herzog says he is not as worried about
                     deceptive advertising as he is about increases in cigarette sales.
                     The tobacco institution says the FTC may be understating
                     its mission.

October: CAB proposes regulation to ban pipes and cigars in aircrafts.
                     The ICC expands the 1974 twenty percent regulation to
                     thirty percent; bus firms requested fifty percent.

September 6:   FTC attempts to force disclosure of sales and advertising
                     data beyond what the industry normally reports to the agency.

1977

April 30:   Cigarette manufacturers refuse to release information to the
                     FTC on sales and/or advertising expenditures and are sued by
                     the FTC.

June 15:   Eastern Airlines, as part of a settlement with the CAB, in
                     which it is fined ten thousand dollars for fourteen specific
                     violations of smoking area regulations, agrees to ban smoking
                     in sixty-five percent of airplane seats.

Appendix B

List of Leading Cigarette Brands by Company

American:	(A)	(B)	R. J. Reynolds:	(A)	(B)
Carlton	1967		Camel		
Half & Half	1964?	1974	Doral	1960	
Hit Parade	1956	1962	More	1975	
Lucky Strike			Vantage	1970	
Montclair	1962	1974	Tempo	1964	1973
Pall Mall			Salem	1956	
Silva Thins	1968		Winston	1955	
Tareyton (Herbert)					

P. Lorillard:			Brown and Williamson:		
Kent			Blair	1960	
New Port	1957		Life	1959	1974
Old Gold			Kool		
Spring	1959		Raleigh		
True	1966		Viceroy		

Liggett and Myers:			Philip Morris:		
Chesterfield			Alpin	1959	
Duke	1959	1968	Benson & Hedges	1959	
Lark	1963		Marlboro	1955	
L & M	1954		Parliment		
Oasis	1957	1968	Philip Morris		
			Paxton	1963	1966
			Virginia Slims	1968	

(A) Year of introduction if introduced after 1954
(B) Year phased out

Appendix C

List of Non-Leading Cigarette Brands by Company

Company	(A)	(B)	(C)	(D)
American				
Brighton	1968	1969	—	111,100
Bull Durham	1967	1974	0.18	1,946,649
Cold Harbor	1967	1968	—	9,100
Colony	1967	1969	0.075	1,122,820
Compass	1967	1968	—	18,100
Double Eights	1968	1969	—	82,400
Fresh	1970	1971	—	2,600
Iceberg	1972	—	0.89	1,531,841
Mayo	1967	1968	—	40,700
Maryland	1970	1973	0.59	245,550
Sobranie	1971	1972	—	38,200
Super M	1974	1974	—	413,192
Tennyson	1966	1969	—	203,240
Twist	1973	1974	0.5	2,673,994
Waterford	1966	1967	0.27	5,900
Brown and Williamson*				
Avalon	—	1966	0.09	—
Breeze	1963	1964	—	9,210
Capri	1967	1970	0.12	51,800
Dover Long	1967	1969	0.045	315,800
Du Maurier	1956	—	0.1	24,241
Fact	1975	—	0.02	274,300
Flair	1970	1972	0.025	92,800
Hallmark	1970	1972	0.1	36,200
Kentucky Kings	1960	1963	0.63	138,150
Lyme Menthol	1971	1973	—	71,500
Sudedes	1975	—	—	86,900
Tramps	1974	—	0.55	790,493
Vanguard	1975	—	—	39,600
Wings	—	1971	0.18	—
Liggett and Myers				
Adam	1971	1975	—	374,866
Devon	1964	1966	0.06	39,312

Eve	1970	—	1.45	2,662,850
Fatima	—	1968	0.22	—
Master Piece	1965	1966	0.75	1,284,880
St. Moritz	1974	—	—	289,617

P. Lorillard

Century Great	1967	1969	—	2,243,270
Davill	1966	1967	0.05	11,100
Embassy	—	1955	0.45	—
Maverick	1971	1974	0.006	84,366
York	1961	1968	0.59	470,135

Philip Morris

Ambasador	1967	1971	—	18,752
Commander	1961	1964	—	1,033,182
Dunhill	—	1956	0.25	—
Galaxy	1965	1974	0.48	67,144
Gauloises	1961	1964	0.06	16,125
Merit	1975	—	—	—
New Leaf	1970	1973	0.13	658,100
Saratoga	1975	—	1.86	8,270,900
Spuds	—	1957	0.13	315,661

R. J. Reynolds

Brandon	1962	1967	0.18	473,480
Cavalier	—	1964	0.92	—
Embra	1969	1971	—	152,358
Mr. Menthol	1970	1971	—	56,200
Now	1975	—	—	8,900

(A) Year of introduction; (—) if introduced prior to 1954.
(B) Year phased out; (—) either sold in 1976 or no data could be obtained.
(C) Average annual sales in billion units; (—) no data could be obtained.
(D) Average annual expenditures on advertising in undeflated dollars; (—)
    no data could be obtained.

* According to *Tobacco Retailer's Almanac,* 1973 Annual Directory to Tobacco
  Candy and Sundries, Retail Tobacco Dealers of America, 1973, Brown and
  Williamson also offer the following non-leading brands: Actron, Barcly, Cali-
  fornia, Cornet, Cougar, Dalton, Daytona, Gresham, Laredo, LeMans, Look,
  Montana, Nashville, Normandy, Pinto, Sierra, Spirit, Today, Tomorrow,
  Triedent, Valiant, Ventora, and Vita Filters. We have no information about
  these brands.

Appendix D

Industry Aggregate Data Utilized in the Tests, 1954-1975

Year	(A)	(B₁)	(B₂)	(C)	(D)	(E)	(F)	(G₁)	(G₂)	(H)
1954	356.7	3013	3266	525319	162239	687558	21.2	.503	.464	.98
1955	375.6	3138	3403	546410	167686	714096	22.6	.496	.457	.99
1956	386.6	3192	3466	816399	179692	996091	22.7	.492	.454	.97
1957	403.4	3284	3578	819770	236059	1055289	22.6	.491	.451	.94
1958	421.6	3384	3696	988990	249386	1238376	22.2	.480	.439	.91
1959	451.1	3598	3946	1164872	281191	1446063	22.0	.449	.409	.91
1960	467.7	3692	4051	969037	289257	1258876	23.2	.471	.429	.89
1961	483.8	3743	4128	979870	260684	1240554	23.0	.462	.406	.88
1962	489.7	3727	4127	910044	288422	1198466	22.8	.450	.406	.87
1963	505.9	3788	4213	1203034	352314	1555348	23.0	.444	.399	.86
1964	493.5	3636	4062	1542650	267710	1810360	23.4	.432	.386	.85
1965	510.0	3697	4119	1410213	280018	1690231	23.2	.402	.361	.84
1966	519.8	3711	4136	1478287	262292	1740579	23.6	.396	.359	.81
1967	525.8	3696	4123	1849998	247405	2107504	24.0	.395	.354	.79
1968	521.7	3606	4028	1501968	300144	1802112	24.4	.392	.351	.76
1969	512.4	3485	3893	1649239	313906	1963145	24.7	.400	.357	.72
1970	520.4	3469	3880	1426756	400639	1827392	25.1	.400	.357	.68
1971	530.7	3470	3883	0000000	1045122	1045122	25.2	.396	.354	.65
1972	546.1	3505	3992	0000000	1331693	1331693	25.1	.386	.345	.63
1973	570.6	3601	4027	0000000	1198479	1198479	24.0	.356	.319	.59
1974	586.2	3640	4067	0000000	1367898	1367898	23.0	.356	.314	.53
1975	591.1	3609	4025	0000000	1282544	1282544	21.9	.338	.302	.49

(A)   Total industry sales of cigarettes, billion units.
(B₁ & B₂)   Sales per capita, population fourteen years and older (B₁), eighteen years and older (B₂), in units.
(C)   Deflated expenditures on television and radio advertising, in hundreds of dollars.
(D)   Deflated expenditures on print advertising, in hundreds of dollars.
(E)   D + C, in hundreds of dollars.
(F)   Average price of a package, in deflated cents (see text).
(G₁ & G₂)   Index of effective price of cigarette package, population fourteen and older (G₁), eighteen and older (G₂), see text.
(H)   Deflator (see text).

Index

73604